TRAILBLAZERS AND TRIUMPHS OF THE GOSPEL

To Richard

Best wishes

James   Nov 2021

TRAILBLAZERS AND TRIUMPHS OF THE GOSPEL

"Making Disciples of all Nations"

Brief accounts of some of those who pioneered with the Gospel in several countries and of some great revivals in recent times

by Bert Cargill and James Brown

RITCHIE
John Ritchie Publishing
40 Beansburn, Kilmarnock, Scotland

ISBN-13: 978 1 912522 40 8

Copyright © 2018 by John Ritchie Ltd.
40 Beansburn, Kilmarnock, Scotland

www.ritchiechristianmedia.co.uk

Typeset by John Ritchie Ltd., Kilmarnock
Printed by Bell & Bain Ltd., Glasgow

Acknowledgements

Many of these accounts have been compiled from information available on websites in the public domain. In addition, individual sources are noted and acknowledged in footnotes throughout the book. The authors are grateful for access to all of these.

They are also extremely grateful to their respective wives for their patience and understanding during many hours of writing, and to Christian friends too many to mention for their stimulus and support over many years.

Contents

2.   *Triumphs of the Gospel*

Preface

The first volume in this series, published in 2017, has recalled the courageous lives and costly convictions of those who brought the light of the Gospel and the truth of God's Word into the darkness of 16th to 18th century Great Britain. That is why we chose to call them **Torchbearers of the Truth**. The spiritual and indeed the social progress of the past 500 years in the UK and elsewhere owes much to these Christians and the great Reformation movement which began in Europe and spread into many regions beyond.

This second book takes the story forward with accounts of some of those who took the Gospel message into some of these "regions beyond". Missionaries ventured far into the unknown, motivated by the love of God and a sense of His call to bring the message of saving grace "into all the world". Many of them gave their lives and their all to do this. We have called them **Trailblazers of the Gospel,** for so they were. You can follow their fascinating stories in the first section of this book.

We have also attempted to describe some of the **Triumphs of the Gospel** during the 19th and 20th centuries in the UK and also in some parts of the USA. Great revivals did happen and thousands of individuals from all walks of life were led into the triumph of the crucified, risen and glorified Christ. The second section of the book contains stirring accounts from these past days when so many found the Gospel to be "the power of God unto salvation to everyone that believes" (Rom 1.16).

As in Volume 1, most of these chapters are edited versions of a series of short articles which first appeared monthly in the *Believer's Magazine* during 2013 to 2016. Other somewhat longer chapters have been freshly written, and all are now collated here for the benefit of a wider readership.

May the fortitude, perseverance and commitment of these pioneering servants of the Lord challenge us who live in an easier and more affluent age. They suffered much "for the Gospel's sake" (1 Cor 9.23). May we be stirred also with a fresh thrill at the evidence of the working of the Holy Spirit in past days. And may we be motivated to seek and pray for a fresh visitation of this divine "power unto salvation" in these darkening and closing days of this dispensation of God's grace in which we are called to live for Christ and be His witnesses before He comes again.

Part 1
TRAILBLAZERS OF THE GOSPEL

"Go therefore and make disciples of all the nations.
baptizing them in the name of the Father
and of the Son and of the Holy Spirit,
teaching them to observe all that I have commanded you:
and lo, I am with you always,
even to the end of the age."

(Mt 28.19-20; NKJV)

Trailblazers and Triumphs of the Gospel

CHAPTER 1

19th Century Britain

Recent centuries have all been marked by great changes, including our present one already. But the changes during the 19th century were so fundamental and far reaching that we are still living in their aftermath more than one hundred years since it closed. From the viewpoint of the UK it is probably still regarded by many as the grand Victorian era. The British Empire was expanding rapidly, "Britannia ruled the waves" and by force or by influence imposed its style upon large parts of the world. Colonial expansion by several European nations was the order of the day particularly in the scramble for possessions in Africa. Whilst many nowadays look back upon it all with some misgiving and even indignation at the exploitation and repression of native peoples, it is nevertheless historical fact. It hugely influenced British society and affected the foreign policy of the major powers of Europe.

At home the Industrial Revolution had well and truly come of age. Powered by steam generated from apparently endless supplies of coal dug out of countless coalmines by strong men labouring in the dark and damp, Britain was "the workshop of the world". Expansion was rapid. Railways, factories, trade, cities, seaports and armed forces and navies grew faster than ever, and for many, wealth increased to match. It was the century of extensive building projects in the cities and grandiose ones in the country, with labour cheap and easy to obtain. But many aspects of Victorian society were truly appalling - the grinding poverty of working men and their large families, the squalor of crowded housing, child mortality at an awful level, rampant immorality and drunkenness, health care hardly invented. "Dark Satanic mills" overshadowed lives and cities.

But the Spirit of God was truly moving in these islands. In the 18th century the "Great Awakening" saw spiritual revivals led by the Wesleys and Whitefield, for example, along with several others described in Volume 1 of this series. Now in the 19th century there was a further and unprecedented expansion of Gospel preaching, a further evangelical awakening which would match the scale of the Reformation and build upon it. The growing towns and cities provided increasing opportunities for the Word of God to be brought to larger crowds than ever. This would be the century when the largest number of mission halls and churches (some to hold thousands) would be built all over the country and filled to capacity, where men of God would hold forth the Gospel of saving grace. True spiritual revivals were experienced in many places, and evocative accounts of some of these can be read later in this book. They were truly "triumphs in Christ" with the Gospel (2 Cor 2.14).

Along with these mighty revivals at home, there was pioneering, literally trailblazing missionary endeavour abroad. Worldwide mission became both relevant and important. Men such as William Carey and David Livingstone were sponsored by Missionary Societies, whilst others such as Anthony Norris Groves went abroad independently as guided by the Holy Spirit. This book describes some of these individuals, and how they took the glorious message of the Gospel from the shores of Britain into totally unknown, primitive and dangerous conditions beyond distant shores. In the providence of God the trading routes of the expanding and prospering British Empire provided the means of travel for such pioneering missionaries. Some of them were the first to translate the Scriptures into the languages of those to whom they went, truly laying the foundation for the many who would follow them. Past and present lists of missionaries from the UK and the USA for example show how fully the passion and example of these trailblazers has been followed ever since.

It is very difficult for us in the comfort of the 21st century with its ready facilities for easy travel, quick communication, and good healthcare to appreciate properly the difficulties and hardships experienced by these intrepid pioneers. And many of them did pay the ultimate price to fulfil their vision, some killed by those they came to reach. Not a few set foot only briefly on the lands of their calling where they succumbed to diseases to which they had no resistance. Many are buried in unknown graves in these distant lands, awaiting a glorious resurrection and well merited reward.

The following chapters have been written in an attempt to honour their memory in some way. May these retold stories of their courageous endeavours to bring the Gospel to others, and the examples of their faithfulness to God, challenge us all once again.

BC

CHAPTER 2

William Carey (1761 - 1834)

The huge subcontinent of India had become a source of much trade and accrued wealth to an ambitious Great Britain in the 18th and 19th centuries, mainly through the trading power of the British East India Company which had been founded in 1600. But it had hardly been touched by the Gospel in the years since British trade and influence had begun. Legends with some foundation tell of the apostle Thomas bringing the Word of God to western parts of India in the 1st century. Now, at the end of the 18th century, a humble man called William Carey became a brave trailblazer of the Gospel into that large country.

It is appropriate that in this book we look at him first, for he has been described as

> the father and founder of modern missions;
>
> cobbler by trade; scholar, linguist and missionary by God's training;
>
> the man who said, 'Expect great things from God - attempt great things for God'.

Early Life

William Carey was born into a weaver's family in a small village near Northampton on 17th August 1761. As a teenager he developed two main interests – exploring the countryside around him learning what he could about nature, and reading tales of adventure. His favourite author was Christopher Columbus whom he quoted so much that his friends nicknamed him "Columbus".

When he was 17 he was apprenticed to a shoemaker at Hackleton along with John Warr, a devout young Christian who showed to him a great concern for his soul. Affected by Warr's spiritual sincerity, he agreed to attend some services at the Dissenters' Church where the Word of God was preached with warmth and conviction. Eventually he abandoned his own self righteousness, was truly converted to Christ, and joined the local Congregational Church. There he married Dorothy Plackett in 1781. She was a devoted wife, though she never shared his great missionary passion, in fact she had a mental illness which dogged the rest of her life.

The newly converted Carey walked five miles to Olney where the teaching of the "Particular Baptists" helped him grow in Christ. He was baptized on 5th October 1783. Two years later he moved to Moulton to become a schoolmaster, and then he became a pastor to a small congregation there.

Missionary Calling

His missionary interest was stirred by reading the *Last Voyage of Captain Cook,* a tale of adventure from nearer his own time than Columbus. But to him it was more than an adventure story - it was a revelation of human need! An avid reader, by now he had grasped Latin, Greek, Hebrew and Italian, and was learning Dutch and French. His cobbler's shop became known as "Carey's College", for he never sat at his bench without some book in front of him.

The more he read the Bible and studied it, the more convinced he was that "the peoples of the world need Christ". He read, he made notes, he constructed a large globe of the world out of scraps of leather. One day, in the quietness of his workplace he read: "If it be the duty of all men to believe the Gospel ... then it be the duty of those who are entrusted with the Gospel to endeavor to make it known among all nations." Carey sobbed out, *"Here am I; send me!"* The text which compelled him was: "Thy Redeemer ... The God *of the whole earth* shall He be called" (Isa 54.5).

His passion for reaching lost souls increased. Often during a geography lesson in his school he pointed to a map of the world and exclaimed, "The people living in these areas are lost, hundreds of millions of them, not knowing the blessed Saviour!" When a neighbour suggested that he preached too often and neglected his shoemaking, he replied, "My real business is to preach the gospel ... I cobble shoes to pay expenses."

But to his dismay he found that others did not share his concerns. When he proposed a discussion on: "Whether the command given to the apostles to teach all nations was not obligatory ... to the end of the world, seeing that the accompanying promise was of equal extent", an older minister shouted, "Young man, sit down: when God pleases to convert the heathen, He will do it without your aid or mine."

On 2nd October 1792, Carey preached a memorable sermon from Isaiah 54.2-3, summarizing it with the words, *"Expect great things from God - attempt great things for God"*. Out of this came the first missionary society in England. Through reports from Mr Thomas, a surgeon with the East India Company, India became his focus. Thomas had started some Gospel work there, but felt the need of more help from home. At one of the Missionary Society meetings someone said, "There is a gold mine in India, but it seems almost as deep as the centre of the earth. Who will venture to explore it?" Said Carey, "I will venture to go down, but remember that you must hold the ropes."

To India

But it was not a simple matter to get to India. The only way there was by the shipping of the East India Company which, even more than the religious establishment, was unsympathetic to missionary endeavour. Also his wife did not want to go with him. After some weeks' delay through a failed attempt to get on a British ship, he obtained passage in the Danish ship *Kron Princessa Maria*, and now his wife Dorothy with their five children was willing to go. They arrived in Calcutta in November 1793 and for seven years moved from place to place while learning the language, experiencing poverty and rejection, fevers and bereavement. Dorothy and two of his children had severe dysentery; five year old Peter died and no one would dig his grave so Carey did it himself. In 1800 he moved to Serampore, a Danish settlement, where he found better acceptance than in the British sector. Dorothy died in 1807. He then married a Danish lady, Charlotte who had been the first European lady to be baptized in India. She died in 1821, and in 1823 he married Grace Hughes.

The numerous difficulties did not hinder him from language study, starting schools, taking missionary tours, and most important to him, translating the New Testament. To support his family he found employment for a time supervising an indigo factory, the owners of which allowed him to set up a printing press in one of its corners. In 1801 Carey was able to say, "I have lived to see the Bible translated into Bengali, and the whole New Testament printed." By 1806, he with others proposed translations into 15 other languages. Competent local men were employed under their guidance and supervision, so that in the space of 25 years, translations of portions of the Old and New Testaments had been made in 40 different dialects. What a task that was providing a secure foundation for future work in India!

His printing work was innovative. First he improved on the native paper which had been prone to insect attack, then he imported a 12 HP steam engine to drive the paper mill. But in 1812 they had a fire which raged for three days. Many manuscripts and materials were destroyed, the result of many years of painstaking work gone up in flames. However, Carey rescued the metal, matrices and punches from the debris, and within two months the printers were again at work. He preached the next Lord's Day from the text, "Be still, and know that I am God". He wrote, "Travelling a road the second time, however painful it may be, is usually done with greater ease and certainty than when we travel it for the first time." A later report tells of 99,000 volumes being printed in nine years, or 31,000,000 pages of Old and New

Testaments. And this was early 19th century India, with a steam driven printing press!

Seven years of patient preaching passed, along with much discouragement, until he saw his first convert, Krishnu. He had come to the mission with a dislocated shoulder, and the kindness he received impressed him. He kept coming, and then one day he cried out, "I am a great sinner! Save me, Sahib!" They pointed him to Christ who alone could save him. He was later baptized, along with Carey's son Felix, aged 15, and he became a faithful servant of God among his own people.

Recognition at last

William Carey was eventually honoured by the British authorities in India. He had established the first poor schools and a leper hospital. He developed agriculture and made seminal studies on the local flora and fauna, and the minerals of the area. Due to his influence, horrible practices like child sacrifice to the River Ganges, and *suti*, the immolation of a widow on her husband's funeral pyre, were banned. He earned a doctorate, and due to his great linguistic abilities he was awarded a professorship at the Government College at Fort William, with a salary of £1500 p.a. He accepted on condition that all of it would be used to further the work of the mission.

Of all the remarkable technical and academic abilities of this servant of God, what stands out is his perseverance and hard work, but equally so do his humility and devotion to Christ. At a dinner one day a somewhat sarcastic military general ventured to ask, "Was not William Carey once a shoemaker?" He overheard the question and replied, "No, sir, only a cobbler." During his last illness, he said to his friend, "Mr. Duff, you have been saying much about Dr. Carey and his work. After I am gone, please speak not of Dr. Carey, but rather of my wonderful Saviour."

He explicitly requested that on his gravestone only his name, the dates of his birth and his death be engraved, and two lines from a hymn:

'A wretched, poor and helpless worm,
On Thy kind arms I fall.'

He died at sunrise on 9th June 1834, and he was laid to rest in the Christian burial ground at Serampore.

BC

CHAPTER 3

Henry Martyn (1781 – 1812)

Some of God's servants have been granted many years to fill with service for Him, others only a few. Henry Martyn was one of these others, along with David Brainerd before him (1718-1747), missionary to the American Indians (see Chapter 19), and Robert Murray McCheyne of Dundee after him (1813-1843). The labours and the influences of such men have lived far beyond their brief lifespans, however.

Martyn served the Lord in India from 1806 to 1810. His was an unpopular and difficult task as we shall see. He had an effective ministry among native Indians though often despised and threatened with violence. But his more lasting legacy was his translation of the Scriptures, enabling the gospel to spread and prosper in that region for decades to come. His love and passion for the Word of God drove him to study it deeply and so to translate it into Hindustani (Urdu) and Persian. This latter language was probably the most widely used in the east at that time, from north India to Persia itself, even used officially in the judicial courts of British governed Hindustan.

Early Background

Henry Martyn was born in Truro, Cornwall, on 18th February 1781, twenty years after William Carey, and ten years before John Wesley died. His father was an early Methodist who had heard Wesley preaching. Henry had a strict upbringing and lived a morally upright life, but as a brilliant young man he pursued academic excellence to the exclusion of a meaningful spiritual life. From Truro Grammar School he went up to St. John's

College, Cambridge in 1797, studied maths, law and the classics, and in 1801 was 'Senior Wrangler' in mathematics - he was the brightest and the best student in his year.

In 1800 his father died. Recognising now his parents' influence and heeding his sister's pleadings he was converted. His life took on a complete change of emphasis. He wrote, "The whole current of my desires is altered, I am walking quite another way." He read the Bible with a new interest, and continued to study languages. He already had a firm grasp of Hebrew, Greek and Latin, and now he was learning Hindustani, Bengali, Persian and Arabic.

From Cambridge he had intended to follow the legal profession, but now he began preparing for the ministry of the Church of England. He came under the influence of Charles Simeon, a man deeply committed to the relatively new missionary ideas in the established church. One area where Simeon actively sought to pursue this was in the powerful East India Company where so far missionaries had been unwelcome in case they upset the good trading prospects of the company. (We have noted this in the case of William Carey.) Martyn was chosen to go to India as a chaplain to the British community in Calcutta, but wider ambitions were burning in his heart and soul.

Into India

He set sail for India in 1805, the year of the Battle of Trafalgar. Because of potential dangers near the coast of Europe, his ship detoured via San Salvador in Brazil and the voyage took twice as long as usual. First he was badly sea-sick, and also lonely and love sick for he had left his sweetheart Lydia Grenfell whom he had hoped to marry. But the nine months at sea gave him time to influence ungodly sailors, to minister to other passengers, and to study his languages and his books. Calling at Cape Town in January 1806, and seeing the dreadful bloodshed of the British conquest of the Cape Colony, his prayer became that *England whilst she sent the thunder of her arms to distant regions of the globe, might ... show herself great indeed, by sending forth the ministers of her church to diffuse the gospel of peace.* At last in May 1806, they landed in Calcutta, and he exclaimed, "Now let me burn out for God!"

He spent his first five months in Serampore and benefited greatly from time with William Carey who developed a high regard for him. His ministry among the British was not much wanted, however. His sermons were too forthright, applying the Gospel call to repentance to all his hearers without distinction. Also his free association with natives of every caste was frowned upon.

He moved out to Dinapore and then to Cawnpore to pursue his greater vision of reaching others. He was deeply distressed by what he saw of the destructive influences of practices in the Hindu and Muslim religions of the country, and he energetically preached Christ crucified and risen again. Daily he repeated his message of repentance toward God and faith in the Lord Jesus Christ until he was often hoarse. He started schools for local children, using as textbooks his newly translated parables from the Gospels in Hindustani or Arabic. He often visited hospitals and read *Pilgrim's Progress* to the sick folk. Enthusiastic though he was for this kind of work, he wrote one day, "Without the work of translation I should fear my presence in India were useless."

Translation Work

While in this eastern region of India he had translated the New Testament and the *Book of Common Prayer* into Hindustani, a spoken language which he was able to put on a firm written foundation for the first time. But he sensed that Persian was a language which would reach many more peoples in the region, and to execute properly that translation he would have to travel to Persia (Iran) itself. This would be a major undertaking.

A six weeks' voyage took him back westwards round the tip of India to Bombay. On 25th March 1811 by agreeing to act as chaplain for the voyage, he got out of Bombay on the *Benares,* an East India Company ship, and arrived in Muscat (Masqat) on the Arabian side of the Gulf of Oman on 21st April. At last he landed at Bushire (Bushehr) on the Persian side a month later. It was then nine days on horseback to Shiraz, some 200 miles into the mountains where was welcomed by Sir Gore Ousley, the British Ambassador.

Shiraz was full of Muslim theologians, clerics and scholars. They were keen to debate with this young foreigner who was always ready to receive them. His wisdom and sincerity endeared him to many, but they could not accept the deity of Jesus Christ. Martyn wrote a series of courteous tracts on this fundamental subject and saw some of these men converted. Meantime he pursued his great objective of completing the Persian New Testament and also translating the Psalms.

On 24th February 1812, the work was finished, ready to be presented to the Shah of Persia. With two specially printed copies he travelled to Tabriz where he hoped the British Ambassador would arrange a personal audience with the Shah. But instead he had a hostile reception from the Shah's Vizier who challenged him to say, "God is God and Mohammed is his Prophet." There was a silence, then Henry Martyn replied, "God is God, and Jesus is the Son of God." A great uproar and melee followed immediately! Mercifully he was just able to escape from the mob uninjured with his precious New Testaments safe. Later, however, the British ambassador was able to present the Persian New Testament to the Shah who actually commended it to his people.

Ill health

Just months later, by September, Martyn's health was deteriorating badly. The ambassador and his wife in Tabriz nursed him devotedly for a time. He got no better so it was decided that he would have to return to England, first 1200 miles overland to Constantinople, there to seek passage home via Malta. On the overland journey he suffered much. Even those he had trusted took advantage of his growing weakness, neglected him and stole from him. As he passed by Mt. Ararat in the distance he thought on Noah, and wrote, "Here the blessed saint landed in a new world; so may I, safe in Christ, outride the storms of life and land at last on one of the everlasting hills."

The last entry in his journal was made on 6th October 1812. "No horses being to be had, I had an unexpected repose. I sat in the orchard and thought with sweet comfort and peace of my God; in solitude my Company, my Friend, and Comforter. When shall appear that new heaven and new earth wherein dwelleth righteousness? There, there, none of that wickedness which has made men worse than wild beasts, none of those corruptions which add still more to the miseries of mortality, shall be seen or heard of any more."

Ten days later Henry Martyn died, aged 31. He was buried in Tokat by members of the Armenian Church. His tombstone tells us -

HE LABOURED FOR MANY YEARS IN THE EAST,

STRIVING TO BENEFIT MANKIND BOTH IN THIS

WORLD AND THAT TO COME.

HE TRANSLATED THE HOLY SCRIPTURES INTO

HINDOSTANEE AND PERSIAN, AND PREACHED

THE GOD AND SAVIOUR OF WHOM THEY TESTIFY.

HE WILL LONG BE REMEMBERED IN THE EAST,

WHERE HE WAS KNOWN AS A MAN OF GOD.

BC

Grateful acknowledgement to C P Hallihan, *Quarterly Record*, 562, 563; Trinitarian Bible Society, 2003, for information used in this chapter.

CHAPTER 4

Adoniram Judson (1788 – 1850)

Judson is remembered as the man who gave the Bible to Burma and who first brought the Gospel to the Karen peoples. All his tasks were carried through at great personal cost and with much suffering, culminating in his eventual death and burial in an unmarked grave.

Unpromising Start

Unlike others whom we are describing in this part of the book, he was American. Born on 9th August 1788 in Malden, Massachusetts, he quickly showed he was a brilliant child, learning to read when he was three years old, and soon mastering mathematics, Latin and Greek at school. In 1804 he went up to Rhode Island College which his father, a strict conservative pastor, believed would be safer for him than the more liberal Harvard. But this did not work out as planned, for by the end of his course he had become a deist, no longer believing in the existence of a personal God or a Saviour. He then went on to New York to join a troupe of travelling actors.

One night while lodging at an inn he was disturbed by strange noises from the next room. He was horrified to discover that these were the dying groans of his college friend, the very one who had influenced him to reject faith in God. The awful fate of an unsaved soul so affected him that he returned to Plymouth to his parents' home. Within three months he was converted, regaining what he had lost for these years. In December 1808 he wrote in his journal: "This day I made a solemn dedication of my life to God." Five months later, now age 20, he joined his father's Congregational Church in Plymouth.

Missionary Calling

While attending Andover Seminary he found a group of young men interested in missions, not only among the native American Indians but much farther afield. As a result, in 1811 a Foreign Missions Board of the Congregational Churches of Massachusetts was formed. First Judson was sent to England to see if cooperation with the London Missionary Society would be possible. During that voyage he was captured by French privateers but escaped. The proposed venture with the LMS was unsuccessful, and after he returned to Plymouth his mentors agreed to his going to Burma 'or elsewhere as…Providence shall open the most favourable door'. In February 1812 he married Ann Hasseltine, and before the end of the month they had set sail from Salem on a small cargo ship, the *Caravan,* for the four months' voyage to Calcutta.

While at sea, another important change occurred in his thinking. He had with him a letter of introduction to William Carey whom he knew was an English Baptist missionary. He got down to studying what the New Testament taught about baptism with the aim of defending his own (congregationalist) views on this ordinance of scripture. But he soon became convinced that believers' baptism was correct and necessary, and Ann agreed with him, though they knew this would cut off all support from their friends at home. Having counted the cost, they were baptized by William Ward, one of Carey's associates, after they arrived in India.

From India to Burma

Once in Calcutta, however, their difficulties multiplied. Not only had they no support from home, but the British East India Company did not want any 'American Missionaries', even more so now that Britain and America were at war again. So they were ordered out of the country. Somehow they found themselves on a ship which landed at Mauritius. Before they reached their destination Mrs Judson had her first baby, but sadly that little one died. On 13th July 1813 they got to Rangoon which they found was a really filthy and corrupt place. They were able to settle in a mission house where Felix Carey had begun a gospel work but had left it to enter government service.

They set about learning Burmese, a complex language which seemed to be an unbroken string of strange characters. Ann became more fluent in everyday speech, whilst Adoniram studied its structure carefully to give him confidence in translation. He saw that the Burmese people already had an extensive literature which they both began to read seriously, and he became even more convinced that the Bible in Burmese was essential for the progress of the Gospel[1]. He obtained a small printing press, and in May 1817 he published his translation of the Gospel of Matthew. He was also compiling a Burmese grammar book, all the while suffering from long illness and also grieving over the death of Roger, their second child, aged seven months.

In 1819, he felt confident enough to begin preaching. In the fashion of the place he erected a *zayat* (a small hut on posts) beside a main road where people could come in and listen to a teacher. In this case it was a Christian one. In June 1819, Judson baptized his first convert, Moung Nau, a labourer, age 35. By 1822 eighteen believers were meeting together in a church setting.

At this time Ann's health was causing great concern. They went back to Calcutta for a few months in 1820, but decided that a spell at home would be best for her. She went during 1822-1823 and recovered. After her return to Rangoon, Adoniram decided that he should visit Ava, the capital of the Burmese empire where was the court of the powerful "Golden Emperor" whom he hoped would grant religious tolerance and allow Christianity to continue in his country.

---

[1]Robert Morrison had the same conviction regarding the Bible in Chinese as will be described in the next chapter.

At first he was favourably received, but a few months later war broke out between the Emperor and the British over a dispute at the Indian border. Foreigners were regarded as spies, and Judson with many others was thrown into prison where he was held for 17 months in appalling conditions. During an eight mile forced march from one prison to another on scorching hot sand and gravel, his feet were so lacerated that he had to be carried at the end. It was only due to his wife Ann's intervention and intercessions to the authorities that he survived these cruel ordeals. She also preserved his precious manuscripts.

More Tragedies

At last they were able to return together to Rangoon in 1826 but there they found anarchy, and the mission property destroyed. They moved the remaining believers to a safer location at Amherst. In September of that year Adoniram was asked back to Ava to help the British negotiate a treaty with the Emperor. During his absence Ann developed fever again and she died on 24th October, aged 37. Adoniram did not receive this news until a month later. He returned to Amherst on 24th January 1827, and exactly three months later his little daughter, Maria Elizabeth also died, just over two years old.

Now followed several months of lonely grief and depression. He felt desolate, as if he had lost everything. However some helpers arrived from America, including George and Sarah Boardman, and a new work was established at Moulmein in the south now under British control, and a permanent church was established. Sadly George died in February 1831. Three years later Adoniram married his widow, a capable schoolteacher. During eleven years together they had five surviving children. He revised his Burmese Bible while continuing mission work in Moulmein and among the Karen people. At times he felt his language work took up too much of his time which he would rather have used for preaching the gospel.

In 1844, Sarah's health was clearly failing, and their return to America was now inevitable. They set sail with three of their older children, but Sarah died at St. Helena[2] in the South Atlantic on 1st September 1845. Judson continued to Boston, by now well known and expected. Although weakened by illness he travelled widely and many listened to him eagerly.

In Philadelphia he met a popular writer, Emily Chubbock. He asked her to write an account of Sarah's life. Then he married her and she became a capable wife and devoted mother to her stepchildren back in Burma, and to their own daughter Emily, born in 1847. Now after 35 years, 23 of them in Moulmein, Judson could rejoice in knowing of over 7,000 Burmans and Karens saved and publicly baptized, and 63 churches established.

The last years of his life were given to writing an English-Burmese dictionary but the work was never completed. He developed a serious lung infection and a sea voyage was prescribed as a cure but he died on board the ship on 12th April 1850, and was buried at sea in the Indian Ocean. Ten days later, unaware of his death, Emily gave birth to a son, Charles, but he died the same day. She later returned to America and died in June 1854.

Adoniram Judson had said, "All missionary operations, to be permanently successful, must be based on the written word." This is how he is best remembered, as his tombstone declares –

MALDEN, HIS BIRTHPLACE.
THE OCEAN, HIS SEPULCHRE.
CONVERTED BURMANS, AND
THE BURMAN BIBLE
HIS MONUMENT.
HIS RECORD IS ON HIGH.

BC

Information for this chapter from several sources, including www.wholesomewords. org and *Quarterly Record*, Trinitarian Bible Society, 2005.

[2]St Helena was then a frequent port of call for passing sailing ships to replenish fresh water supplies and allow passengers to go ashore.

CHAPTER 5

Robert Morrison (1782 – 1834)

Robert Morrison was the very first protestant missionary to China. His abiding legacy is the first translation of the scriptures into the complicated language of this most populous nation on earth. He spent 27 years there, with only one visit home to England. Before leaving for China the first time, a shipping agent asked him if he expected to have any spiritual impact on the Chinese. He answered, "No sir, but I expect God will!"

He was born in Bullers Green, near Morpeth, the youngest son of the eight children of James Morrison, a Scottish farm labourer, and Hannah Nicholson, an English woman, whom he had married in 1768. In 1785 the family moved to Newcastle where his father found work in the shoe trade.

Conversion and Call

When he was twelve, Robert could recite all of Psalm 119 from memory, word perfect! He left school at 14 and entered his father's business, making wooden shoe trees. But he fell into bad company, disregarding his Christian upbringing, and occasionally indulged in drink, until at the age of 16 he was (in his own words) "awakened to a sense of sin … and brought to a serious concern about my soul" and was truly saved.

Manual labour was 12 - 14 hours a day but he found time to read his Bible, usually lying open on his work bench. He also read *The Evangelical Magazine* and *The Missionary Magazine*, becoming deeply interested and wanting to get involved in such work. But his parents opposed this and he promised his mother that he would not go abroad as long as she lived. He started learning Latin, Greek and Hebrew as well as systematic theology and shorthand. He regularly visited the sick, taught poor children, and was greatly concerned for the conversion of his friends and family. In January 1803 he began training as Congregationalist minister in London.

He cared for his mother in her last illness, and before she died in 1804 she gave him her blessing to go abroad. He applied to the London Missionary Society, was accepted at once, and took further training in Gosport. He was torn between Africa and China as possible fields of service, and prayed that "God would station him in that part of the missionary field where the difficulties were greatest and to all human appearances the most insurmountable".

It was China that Morrison was led to. He wrote to a friend, "I wish I could persuade you to accompany me. Take into account the 350 million souls in China who have not the means of knowing Jesus Christ as Saviour…" In London he studied medicine and astronomy, and also began to learn Chinese from a student with whom he shared lodgings. He rapidly made progress in speaking and writing this extremely difficult language.

The Challenge of China

On 31st January 1807 Robert Morrison set sail on the first leg of his journey to China. The voyage was to New York on the *Remittance* through many stormy seas. After a month there he boarded another ship, the *Trident*, bound for Macau, having secured the goodwill of the American Consul at Canton. He would need this, for all foreigners entering China were interrogated as to their purpose and business. If the authorities were not satisfied, they were sent away on the next ship. Chinese people were absolutely forbidden to deal with foreigners except for trading purposes.

After 113 days at sea, the *Trident* arrived in Macau[3]. He was kindly received by Englishmen and Americans, but they warned

---

[3]Macau was a Portuguese administered settlement and trading port on the South China coast about 40 miles from Hong Kong. It became a Special Administered Region (SAR) of China on 20th December 1999.

him of great obstacles in the way of his mission. Firstly, the government forbade Chinese people to teach their language to anyone, under penalty of death. Secondly, no one could remain in China except for trading purposes. Thirdly, established Roman Catholic missionaries were bitterly hostile and in fact expelled him from Macau. Some American factory owners at Canton took him in while he gave himself to language study, but he could not leave his books in the open in case his mission was discovered. He wanted to become fluent in the dialect of the common people, not the Mandarin of a comparatively small aristocratic class.

His trials and discouragements were great, living in almost complete seclusion. His Chinese teacher and servants cheated and robbed him. He tried to live like one of them, but the food and bad housing told on his health. His finances became precarious and prospects seemed cheerless. Political troubles between Britain and China also increased, and foreigners such as he were increasingly under suspicion. The infamous and disgraceful "opium wars" were soon to come, where gunship might would be on the side of Britain and moral right on the side of China. Further progress of the Gospel into that country would be badly jeopardised for some time to come.

He was able to return to Macau in June 1808, but to miserable lodgings at an exorbitant price. He toiled on at his Chinese dictionary, in his private prayers pouring out his soul to God in broken Chinese to help him master the native tongue. His prayers were answered in a remarkable way when a year later he was appointed translator to the East India Company with a salary of £500 a year. Now with some security he continued his mission – translation work increased his familiarity with the language, and gave more opportunity for conversation with the Chinese.

Chinese Bibles

In 1812 his Chinese grammar was finished. It became a pivotal piece of work for enabling England and America to understand China. He sent it to Bengal for printing, but he heard nothing about it for three long years. He went on to print a tract and a catechism, and to translate the Acts and the Gospel of Luke – all of which the Roman Catholic bishop ordered to be burned as heretical. When the Chinese authorities read some of his works, they declared it a capital crime to print and publish Christian books in Chinese. Aware of what this meant, Morrison forwarded a translation of their edict to England, at the same time announcing that he purposed to go forward quietly and resolutely.

To avoid the restrictions in China, he went to Malacca and established an Anglo-Chinese College where printing and training would be done to promote evangelism in the east in years to come. He also wrote home, urging people to learn Chinese, a language, he said, which is the speech of about one-third of mankind. "Tens of thousands of English boys and girls are taught dead languages. Surely some can learn this living one, and so be enabled to make known the Christian faith in the many lands where it is spoken."

In 1814 the first Chinese believer, Tsae A-Ko, was baptised and a local church was begun. Also the Bible Society financed the printing of the New Testament, and a director of the East India Company bequeathed to him $1000. He used this to produce a pocket size New Testament. This was suitable for hiding among the belongings of the many Chinese people who travelled into the interior. After more years of work the whole Chinese Bible was printed.

Family life

In 1809, he had married Mary Morton in Macau, but she died of cholera on 10th June 1821 when Robert was 39. Their position was always dangerous and lonely, and Mary's short married life held much anxiety. Their first child, James, died at birth on 5th March 1811, and in deep sorrow Robert himself had to bury the little one on a mountainside. They had two more children, Mary (July 1812), and John (April 1814).

He returned to England in 1824, and was made a Fellow of the Royal Society. He presented his Chinese Bible to King George

IV, and became greatly respected. He taught Chinese to some of the upper classes, stirring up interest and sympathy on behalf of China and its people. Before returning there he married Eliza Armstrong in November 1824, with whom he had five more children. The new Mrs. Morrison and the children from his first marriage returned with him to China in 1826 where he saw further expansion of his pioneering work for God in that land.[4]

On 1st August 1834 this pioneer missionary to China died at the age of 52 in his son's arms at his residence in Hong Kong and was buried in Macau beside his first wife and child.

He had written to the London Missionary Society: "I know that the labours of God's servants in the gloom of the dungeon have often illuminated succeeding ages, and I am cheered with the hope that my labours in my present confinement will be of some service to the millions of China."

What a great service it was and what a great heritage millions did receive! Although the Cultural Revolution of the 20th century banned the Bible, in the last 25 years no less than 100 million Bibles have been printed in the Amity Press at Nanjing. More than 60 million of these have been for China itself, yet not enough to satisfy the current demand.

BC

---

[4]More details available from C P Hallihan in *Quarterly Record*, Trinitarian Bible Society, 585, Oct 2008.

CHAPTER 6

Anthony Norris Groves (1795 – 1853)

No account of trailblazers of the Gospel would be complete without taking proper notice of the works and ways of Anthony Norris Groves. For good reason he has been called "father of faith missions".

Other chapters in this book describe some of the men who pioneered in India, China and Africa before and after Groves. They were sponsored and supported by Missionary Societies at home. Groves was different. Without any guaranteed salary or support, he left a prosperous and promising lifestyle in England to go first to Baghdad in Persia, then to India. He believed that God had sent him, and his policy was to trust in God alone to supply all he needed. His example has inspired and influenced many to this day.

London and Plymouth

Norris Groves was born in Newton Valence, a village in Hampshire on 1st February 1795, the only boy among five sisters. His father owned a salt-refining business which later collapsed due to unfair competition. He also lost all his savings when a ship in which he had invested was wrecked with 800 men on board. The family learned that security and happiness do not depend on money, a lesson that Norris never forgot.

After schooling locally then at nearby Lymington, he was sent to Fulham near London for secondary education when he was eleven. He lodged with his father's sister and her husband who had a prosperous dentist's practice in the city. After leaving school he briefly studied chemistry before beginning an apprenticeship with his uncle. In addition to dentistry he learned some surgery and medicine at the London hospitals. During these years he attended church as a formality - during the sermons he would read a novel hidden inside the Prayer Book. He had little grasp of the Gospel, had occasional serious aspirations to religion but he was more attracted to the pleasures of the big city.

His cousin Mary Thompson became his friend. She was more seriously religious and they often spoke of spiritual things. One of his first presents to her was a Bible. Friendship developed into serious attachment and courtship. Her mother was sympathetic, but her father was definitely not! He did not believe that his apprentice could provide for his daughter the lavish lifestyle she had known, and he had further reservations about Norris's father's inefficient use of wealth.

Disappointed, Norris moved away to Plymouth where at the age of 18 he set up his own dental practice. It prospered and he hoped Mary's father would now be persuaded to change his mind about their future together. Deep despair followed another abrupt refusal. He grieved more to hear that his beloved Mary was now quite ill. To find some solace he attended the parish church in Plymouth where two evangelical ministers opened his understanding of the way of salvation through faith in Christ alone - his conversion is dated to early in 1816. Now he began to think differently and offered his services to the Church Missionary Society in fulfilment of an earlier aspiration. He wanted to do something for God, but still lacked assurance of acceptance with God.

Meantime things were changing in Mary's home - she was constantly nursing her very ill sister who died soon after. This and the thwarting of her love for Norris brought on such despair that her father at last changed his mind and gave his consent to their marriage which was happily celebrated later in 1816. Her illness and melancholy were immediately cured, and the young couple were overjoyed. By 1822 two boys, Henry and Frank, then a girl, Mary, had been born into their family.

At Exeter

They moved to Exeter in 1820 where business flourished in Northernhay, the large house they bought. His income soon reached £1500 per annum (x 100 at least in today's terms), but his previous interest in foreign missions began to reassert itself. He wrote, "I had a wife who loved me, dear little children, and a most lucrative profession, yet I had not the Lord's presence as in days past, and therefore I was miserable." As he read his Bible he was constantly challenged by its perspective on wealth. The teaching of Christ was about laying up treasure in heaven, using what a man had for the benefit of others. He resolved to follow that course.

Together he and Mary who was reluctant at first, decided to give a tenth of their income to the Lord, then they increased this to a quarter. Ultimately, they agreed that they would live frugally and give the entire surplus to the Lord's work. He laid out his convictions in a booklet written in 1825 called *Christian Devotedness* with the subtitle *The consideration of our Saviour's Precept: Lay not up for yourselves treasures on earth.* It would have significant influence upon many others for years to come. One such was George Muller who would marry Norris's sister Mary in 1830.

In 1826 Groves again offered himself to the Church Missionary Society. They were keen to have him, and Persia was in their sights, but they would not accept him until he was ordained as a clergyman. So he travelled to Dublin to study for the ministry at Trinity College. There he found some believers meeting in a home, including John Parnell, Edward Cronin and John G Bellet. Groves enjoyed their fellowship as they broke bread and united in prayer. His attachment to the Church of England was loosening, something which had already been happening in Exeter through his contact with two godly women, Bessie and Charlotte Paget, dissenters, who had helped him into the real assurance of salvation.

Between two of his trips to Dublin, his wife suggested to him that he did not need to be ordained if God had called him. But he said he had set aside £40 for his next journey and would think about that later. At 3am during that night he was startled to find that thieves had broken into his house and stolen the £40, but that another £16 which he had saved to pay tax was untouched. He saw in this the guiding hand of God and he did not return to take his exams. He wrote, "We spent one of the happiest Sundays I ever recollect, in thinking of the Lord's goodness, in so caring for us to stop our way up, when He does not wish us to go." He now felt free from what he called "the bondage of ecclesiasticism". For the rest of his life his purpose was to practise what the New Testament taught in everything. He learned he should be baptized, causing some of his contemporaries to accuse him of joining a new denomination. He denied that, saying that he wanted simply to be known as a Christian with no other label attached.

In 1828 he left his dental practice, giving it to a younger relative, and they went to live with the Paget sisters. But a sore blow came when their five year old Mary became sickly and died. Just before that, his father in law died, but not before altering his will to bequeath to them over £10,000. This might have seemed like God's provision for foreign travel and new experiences, but they saw it differently. They gave it all away to support the work of the Lord. They recalled that their Saviour was rich, but for our sakes He became poor. They had no doubt that as they trusted Him He would supply all they needed when they needed it. He wrote, "What is the 'glorious liberty of the children of God' but to be dependent only upon One 'who giveth liberally and upbraideth not'." He said, "The Christian's motto should be *Labour hard, consume little, give much, and all to Christ*". Never has anyone more completely practised what he preached.

To Baghdad

On 12th June 1829 the Groves family along with five others set sail from Gravesend on the large yacht *Osprey* bound for St Petersburg, the first leg of their long journey eastwards. This was organized by John Parnell whom he had met in Dublin, and who later became Lord Congleton. The owner of the yacht, Mr Puget, was about to sell it, but agreed with Parnell to make a last trip - free of charge! But it was not free of stormy weather and seasickness! However, this did not stop them from having regular times of Bible study and prayer each day on the deck with the yacht's crew. After a call at Copenhagen for repairs they reached St Petersburg, thankful for the Lord's provision for them thus far. They found believers there, receptive and interested in their mission.

Next it was overland by horseback or in hard carriages with no springs, travelling on primitive roads across Russia, through the Caucasus and into Mesopotamia, arriving at Baghdad on 6th December. They survived frequent breakdowns and delays, often faced with robbers and quarrelsome people. Accommodation when it could be found was frugal and unwelcoming, too cold at night, too hot during the day. They did not have enough money to complete the journey, but the Lord provided for them during those unimaginably tiring and hazardous six months.

Baghdad on the wide flood plain of the Tigris was a well known stop on the trade route from India. An official of the British East India Company in Baghdad provided the first accommodation for the newcomers, but Groves soon decided it was better to get close to the local people and they moved to a house in the centre of the city. Here he opened a boys' school, gave free dental treatment, operated on eye cataracts (yes, he did!), and taught himself Arabic. But they faced much suspicion from the mixed population of Muslims, Jews, Armenian Orthodox and Roman Catholics whose beliefs were seriously confused. Groves wrote, "The difficulties of absolute falsehood are as nothing to those of perverted truth." The task ahead was gigantic, but Groves pressed on with his vision to make Christ known.

Just over a year later, a serious outbreak of the plague and cholera reached Baghdad. Unlike others, Groves decided they would stay in the city where thousands were dying. With appropriate precautions he hoped the disease would not reach them, but sadly it did and first his beloved wife Mary and then their baby girl born in Baghdad died. Added to this disaster, the river Tigris flooded and demolished 7,000 houses, the city was besieged and the ruling Pasha was overthrown by rival Arabs. Two thirds of the population of 80,000 perished. Groves himself fell victim to typhus fever to the point of death. How much more could he endure?

Over these months he had no support from England, and friends who were due to join him had not arrived. His faith was sorely tried during the isolation, but he testified to the faithful provision of the Lord all the time. Eventually letters did arrive, and so did his friends who engaged in further work among the needy souls in Baghdad. Groves needed a break, but he would not go to England. He left Baghdad for India, alone, on 21st May 1833, feeling called to a land that had been on his mind before he had considered Baghdad. Sad to say, by the end of 1834 nothing remained of the mission in Baghdad due to further outbreaks of the plague and the hostility of the locals.

To India

Groves arrived in Bombay in July 1833. He then spent the last 20 years of his life in India except for two visits to England. On his first visit home in 1835 he married Harriet Baynes and they had three children. They returned to India in 1836 with a fresh group of workers and were welcomed especially among the expatriate community. William Carey and Henry Martyn had died shortly before, but the fruit of their work remained.

Groves disliked the evident segregation of wealthy Europeans and poor Indians. He said, "The further I go, the more I am convinced that the missionary labour in India, as carried on by Europeans, is altogether above the natives; nor do I see how any abiding impression can possibly be made, till they mix with them in a way that is not now attempted." He constantly urged missionaries to live more simply, to break their links with all societies, and rely on the Lord alone to supply their need, but few agreed with him. One Indian convert, John Arulappan, became an itinerant evangelist and saw much blessing - Indians responded better to the Gospel when an Indian Christian brought it to them.

Groves and his colleagues became deeply concerned about the plight of converted Hindus – driven out of their families with no chance of a home or a family of their own or a job in an already fragile economy. To provide for such, in 1841 they began a farm stocked with mulberry trees to raise silkworms. It was a great success financially. He was then offered a substantial loan to allow the business to expand, and against his better judgement, Groves went ahead with it. But disease wiped out the silkworms, and after four years it all collapsed leaving Groves in debt. To pay it off he attempted other agricultural work which did succeed in the long term. Meantime he bought a cheap consignment of local sugar to send to England, but before it reached there the market collapsed. He blamed himself for all the mishaps, and introspectively spoke of himself as a "poor cumberer of the ground". He felt these were "years that the locust had eaten".

In 1848 he made his second trip to England, leaving his sons Frank and Henry in charge of some of the more successful enterprises. The voyage home was in a steamer he described as "a complete Noah's ark, crowded with living creatures". Reunion with his wife and family, and old friends, cheered him greatly, but he was deeply dismayed to find serious and irreparable divisions among assemblies in Bristol and Plymouth. He was glad to be going back to India accompanied by his wife Harriet who bore him a baby girl in 1850.

He found now that many Indians had been saved and baptised, as many as 30,000 in one area. He re-opened his English school and continued his ministry among high caste as well as low, teaching from the Acts the principles of church practice and ministry. His later years were much more fulfilling.

By the start of 1852 his health was giving concern - he had intense pain after eating. There was no improvement and he sailed to England again on 14th August without Harriet. He was warmly welcomed in the Muller's home at Bristol and was able to travel and preach at a few assemblies. There he taught the scriptural duty of believers to support those who served the Lord looking to Him alone for their support. As he became weaker he was lovingly cared for, his last days quiet and serene and occupied with Christ. He died on 20th May 1853 from stomach cancer, and was buried in Arno's Vale, Bristol.

His legacy is not large numbers of converts and assemblies. He was not discouraged if only a few responded. He believed that it was his responsibility to preach and the Lord would give the increase. His legacy is in the example of his humility and the life of faith which he lived to the full.

BC

Information in this chapter abstracted from the detailed biography, *Father of Faith Missions*, Robert R Dann, Authentic Media, 2004; gratefully acknowledged.

CHAPTER 7

Robert Moffat (1795 – 1883)

In the context of missionary exploration in Africa, Robert Moffat's name is less familiar to most people than that of David Livingston, his son-in-law (see next chapter). But it was Moffat who really was the pioneer Scottish missionary into southern Africa. The expansion of missions work in southern Africa over the past 150 years really started with him. We can trace this in two important areas.

First, it was Moffat's reports of the deep spiritual needs of the people in southern Africa which stirred and motivated Livingstone to go there, opening up much of the country for others. Livingstone in turn informed and motivated others in a long chain – through Fred Stanley Arnot to Dan Crawford, thence to Robert Allison and George Wiseman, leading on to present day mission work in Angola and Botswana on the one hand, and on the other to Willie Lammond and Zambia, to name but a few.

Second, and of no less importance, he was the first to translate the Bible into one of the Bantu languages of southern Africa, a critically important task. In spite of very limited education in early life, he learned Dutch among the Boers, then Setswana among the people of the Kalahari Desert so that he could communicate with those people to whom he had been sent. After years of painstaking labour he produced the Setswana New Testament in 1838 then the whole Bible in 1857. A revision of his translation is still widely used in Botswana today.

Early Background

Robert Moffat was born in December 1795 in the village of Ormiston, some 10 miles east of Edinburgh.[5] His father was a Customs-house officer, so they moved to different places a few times during the early years of his life, including Portsoy, Carronshore and Inverkeithing. His parents taught him to pray and read the Bible, and to learn the 'Shorter Catechism'.

His schooling was disjointed due to the various moves, and after 6 months at Falkirk he ran away to sea when he was just 11 years old. Aged 14 he returned home a wiser lad, and found work as a gardener at Polmont near Falkirk, and then at Donibristle in Fife. He would start work at 4am summer and winter for very little pay. After a year in Fife he went south to High Leigh in Cheshire for better pay and conditions, then moved to Dukinfield at the nursery garden of James Smith who had come from Perthshire. Before he left home he promised his mother that he would read a chapter of the Bible every morning. He kept his promise.

At Dukinfield, Wesleyan Methodists befriended him and invited him to some of their meetings nearby. As a result he was convicted of his sin, and after a long struggle he found pardon and peace through faith in Christ. A changed man, he now wanted to devote his life to the service of his Lord and Saviour. After a missionary meeting in Manchester which had moved him greatly, he applied to the London Missionary Society, and he was ordained in Surrey Chapel at the age of 20 along with eight other young missionaries. One of these was John Williams who would go to the Pacific (see Chapter 13), and Moffat wanted to go there with him. But an old Scottish minister vetoed it with the words: *"Thae twa lads are ower young to gang thegither."*

So it would be somewhere else – South Africa. In October

---

[5]His memorial at Ormiston erected in 1885 contains a later tribute by Field Marshal Smuts "Among missionaries there was none greater, none holier than he".

1816, Robert Moffat boarded the *Alacrity* bound for Cape Town, arriving in January 1817. Before leaving England he had become engaged to Mary Smith, his last employer's daughter. She wished to accompany him, but her parents objected. Three years later she did come and they were married in Cape Town. Mary's health was never robust but she supported him capably for the rest of her life.

Southern Africa

Between 1817 and 1819 Moffat travelled through the new turbulent British Cape Colony. He became renowned as a peacemaker while he preached among warring Boers, Zulus, Bushmen, Bantus and Hottentots, though with little impact. But change came when Africaner, chief of the Hottentots, a notorious rebel with a reward of £300 on his head, was truly converted, to the amazement of the authorities. On seeing him, a pious old Boer farmer exclaimed, "O God, what a miracle of Thy power! What cannot Thy grace accomplish?"

Around 1821, with Mary he made the arduous journey to Kuruman in Bechuanaland (now Botswana), south of the great Kalahari Desert. Their little girl Mary was born during the journey. At the start of this new phase of his work, the reception he received was a hostile one. The witchdoctor frequently blamed him for causing droughts (in the desert!). One day soon after they had tried to settle down, the chief arrived with armed men and told him to get out. Mary with their baby in her arms watched him as he faced the menacing chief with his spear in his hand. Moffat opened his shirt and said, "Now then, if you will, drive your spear to my heart; when you have slain me, my companions will know that the hour has come for them to depart." With a shake of his head the chief turned to his men and said, "These men must have ten lives when they are so fearless of death. There must be something in immortality."

After ten years Moffat could speak their language fluently and eventually they came to trust him. But he was greatly burdened because all his work seemed to be in vain. One Sunday he poured out his heart to God in prayer. When he began preaching, the burden of his soul reached out to his hearers. Strong men's eyes filled with tears, many repented and turned to Christ. A new, larger church was opened in May 1829. On the first Sunday of July, six natives were baptised and twelve shared the Lord's Supper that evening. In 1831 a printing press was brought to Kuruman. It would be well used in the coming years.[6]

King Mosilikatse, chief of the Matabele tribe to the east of Kuruman, sent for Moffat to preach to them. He said: "You have made my heart as white as milk. I cannot cease to wonder at the love of a stranger." But Moffat could not stay. He was needed at Kuruman and his priority, translation work, was pressing. He visited the Matabele again in 1835 and King Mosilikatse did all he could to facilitate his preaching. But soon afterwards the Matabeles were driven north by the Zulus and contact was lost for about 20 years.

Scotland and Back

In 1839 Moffat took his first furlough. While he was in London publicizing his book, *Missionary Labours and Scenes in Southern Africa,* David Livingstone met him and it was through that encounter that his interest in Africa was aroused. The Moffats returned to Cape Town in April 1843, and trekked on to Kuruman where they were welcomed by Livingstone who, following the confirmation of his call to Africa, had been there since 1841. He had brought with him 500 copies of Moffat's Setswana New Testament which had been printed in England. Livingston married their daughter Mary in 1845.

In 1853 Moffat found the Matabeles settled away north near the River Zambezi. Mosilikatse was now an old man, and unable to walk. Moffat was able to get him on his feet again and had the opportunity of preaching the Gospel to his people. Moffat's journey was actually to bring provisions to Livingstone and his

---

[6]This press can still be seen with other artifacts in a small museum at Kuruman.

family who had moved there by then but the goods did not reach them until a year later, after 20 Matabele tribesmen had carried them another 150 miles farther north.

After Livingstone's first return to England, the London Missionary Society decided to send out expeditions to the Matabele and to the Makololo, on the north side of the Zambezi. In 1857, Moffat at the age of 62, was asked to lead that expedition to the Matabele. This involved a long journey of 700 miles through very difficult bush terrain. But in this way a work for God was begun at Inyati, led by some new missionaries, among whom was Moffat's own son John.

Latter Years in England

The Moffats suffered many severe trials. In 1862 their oldest son Robert died, about the same time as their daughter Mary, David Livingstone's wife. In 1865, Moffat himself was attacked by an angry native to the danger of his own life. Then his son-in-law, a French missionary Jean Fredaux, was killed tragically, leaving a widow (Ann) and seven needy children. After 50 years' service the LMS wanted him home as his health was failing. So on 20th March 1870, he preached for the last time in Kuruman. Three months' journey overland brought them to Cape Town, and six months later by ship to England to be welcomed by their daughter Helen whom they had not seen for 27 years.

But Mrs Moffat felt a stranger in the land of her birth. She kept remembering her real home in the African sun, so different from dismal, foggy England, and her people in Africa who were much more loving and lovable than these distant English people. There she had been mother to them all; here she was a strange old woman with few friends! Within six months she caught cold and died after a short illness.

Robert Moffat, now a patriarchal figure with a flowing white beard, spoke frequently to large crowds of people, young and old, graphically describing his many experiences in Africa. He received many honours, including special audiences with Queen

Victoria and several eminent statesmen. In 1874 when the body of David Livingstone was brought to England, he escorted it to London and attended the grand funeral service in Westminster Abbey.

On Thursday evening, 9th August 1883, in a little house in Brixton, this pathfinder for missionaries into southern Africa, died at the age of 87 and was buried beside his wife in Norwood Cemetery, London. He had become known as "Moshete of the Bechuanas", the friend of the great king Mosilikatse of the Matabeles, and of Cetewayo of the Zulus. He is perhaps remembered more now as the father-in-law of David Livingstone, but he is the respected spiritual father of many others in southern Africa.[7]

BC

---

[7]More details of this remarkable story at www.wholesomewords.org/missions/ bmoffat3.html

CHAPTER 8

David Livingstone (1813 – 1873)

It is now over 200 years since David Livingstone was born in Blantyre, mid-Scotland, and there must be very few people who have not heard or read of this great trailblazer, explorer and missionary into 'darkest Africa'. Over the past 150 years his story has filled many books, beginning with his own classic, *Missionary Travels and Researches in South Africa* (John Murray, 1857). Sad to say, some recent authors have tended to play down and undermine his Christianity (a sad but common modern trend), and have tried to exaggerate his faults, which doubtless he had. He knew this himself, for he wrote, "God had an only Son, and He was a missionary and a physician. A poor, poor imitation of Him I am or wish to be." After commenting on those obsessive and determined traits of his character, and his poor judgement which had some tragic outcomes, one modern author has redressed the balance by writing, "But this picture, while accurate, does not tell the entire story. Christian faith for Livingstone was the cornerstone of his work in Africa and it permeated every thought and deed. Ultimately Livingstone worked for and with the African peoples."[8]

Such a man and his service for God in the middle of remote, unexplored 19th century Africa must not be forgotten today, or his sacrificial work and his deep motivation underestimated.

---

[8] D Harrison in *David Livingstone - Man, Myth and Legacy*, Ed S Worden, National Museums of Scotland, 2012, p 77.

Scottish Background

Born on 19th March 1813, he was the second eldest son in the family of Neil Livingstone and Agnes (Hunter). They lived in 'one end' in a tenement in Shuttle Row, Blantyre, beside a huge cotton mill powered by the waters of the river Clyde. His grandparents had come to mid-Scotland from the small island of Ulva, close to Mull on the west coast, with the prospect of employment and better living conditions in the prospering industrialised central Scotland. Their father Neil was a travelling tea-salesman, and to supplement his meagre income his three boys were put to work in the cotton mill.

From the age of ten, David was employed in the mill from 6am to 8pm with the hazardous task of tying together broken threads, crawling underneath the fast, noisy cotton spinning machinery, working in temperatures above 90°F. After work he and other youngsters had two more hours at the mill company's school, learning to read and write.

He became a keen reader, never missing an opportunity to get hold of reading material. He would read at home until midnight or when his mother removed his book. At work he would have a book propped up at the spinning frames so that he could catch a few sentences as he passed. He wanted to learn, and he taught himself Latin, then maths and botany. His father, a staunch Calvinist, tried to limit his reading and restrain his curiosity into science (which might undermine faith, he feared), and also terrified him lest he were not one of "the Elect" and so be unable to benefit from the "Limited Atonement".

But when he was 19, a book by Thomas Dick, a nonconformist minister and amateur astronomer, opened his eyes in more ways than one. He found that salvation was available to all who would believe and receive Christ. He also found that science did not undermine faith but rather confirmed God's existence and creative power. Livingstone wrote: "I saw the duty and inestimable privilege immediately to accept salvation by Christ. Humbly believing that through sovereign grace and mercy I have been enabled to do so, it is my desire to show my attachment to the cause of Him who died for me by devoting my life to His service." His father also had a change of heart and of doctrine at this time and the family joined an independent Congregational Church in nearby Hamilton.

By then David had become a qualified cotton spinner in the mill. Four years later he had earned enough money (£12) for the fees of his first year at the medical school of the Andersonian University, Glasgow. He studied mathematics, chemistry, anatomy and surgery[9]. He did this because he had read about a need for missionaries to China, especially those who had a medical training. He wrote: "The salvation of men ought to be the chief desire and aim of every Christian." He also studied Greek and theology under Ralph Wardlaw, an anti-slavery campaigner. Outwith the university terms he continued working at the mill to finance his studies.

But how was it that a poor lad from industrial Lanarkshire should go to darkest Africa? Moved by its great challenge, and out of devotion to Christ, he would not only go, but actually open up a vast swathe of the 'Dark Continent'. There he would make three epic journeys of thousands of miles, most of these on foot, sometimes by canoe, exploring totally unknown regions, observing, recording, drawing maps in his own hand. Perhaps his most remarkable journey was during 1852 to 1856 when he travelled 5,000 miles first from Cape Town in the south to Luanda on the west coast, and then across the continent to the mouth of the Zambesi on the east coast. He would bring home appalling tales of the cruel, ignominious Arab slave trade and this information would propel efforts to abolish it. Most important of all, he would bring the Gospel of Christ to thousands who had never heard it, and open up the way for others to follow his example in years to come.

---

[9]His class certificates can be seen today in the Centre bearing his name in Blantyre. It is well worth a visit. On either side of a cross you read: THE LOVE OF CHRIST CONSTRAINETH US - ST PAUL: THE LOVE OF CHRIST COMPELLED ME - DAVID LIVINGSTONE.

To Africa

During his second year at university he applied to the London Missionary Society and in 1838 began further studies in theology at Chipping Ongar in Essex with China in his mind. But by then the infamous 'Opium Wars' with China had begun, so the LMS directed him towards the West Indies. Early in 1840, however, he met and listened to a Scotsman called Robert Moffat just home from Africa (see previous chapter), telling how he had seen "the smoke of a thousand villages where no missionary has ever been". His heart was stirred, and with this new vision he sought more medical and surgical experience in London. He collected his degree from Glasgow in November 1840, and then on 8th December set sail from Southampton on the *George.* Three months later he landed at Port Elizabeth in South Africa.

His first journey from the coast took over six weeks by cumbersome oxcart, travelling 600 miles north to Kuruman where Moffat had been living. Later he would travel 350 miles farther north to Kolobeng. In 1845 he married the Moffats' daughter Mary. At Kolobeng in a corner of rural Botswana can still be seen the site of their first house, and his 'dentist's chair' - a great square stone at the doorway! There is also a little graveyard where their two-week old baby Elizabeth is buried beside two other explorers. It is a sad, evocative place, the thorn bushes and thickets still difficult to penetrate, little changed since they lived there.

Mary Livingstone is largely forgotten. She had perilous pregnancies (and one miscarriage) due to the long arduous journeys they undertook. In 1852 she returned to Britain with their three surviving children, but sad to say she was very poorly provided for, and in her desperation her faith seems to have wavered. In 1856 Livingstone returned to Britain to write about his travels and to give many lectures, and he gained huge popularity. In 1858 Mary returned to Africa with him and bore him another daughter[10]. Then during a journey to the Zambezi in

---

[10]Their sons were Robert (died 1865 fighting in the American Civil War), Oswell, and Thomas, and surviving daughters Agnes and Anna Mary.

1862 she died of fever and was buried at Chupanga. He visited Britain again in 1864 and returned to Africa in 1866 via Bombay.

Travels and Hardships

Livingstone's travels, determined ambitions, graphic accounts of slavery, and his subsequent fame are well documented and have to be read about in detail elsewhere[11]. He said, "I will go anywhere - provided it be forward." One of his elusive objectives was to find the source of the river Nile. He would be the first white man to see (discover is not the right word) the mighty falls on the River Zambezi, locally called *the smoke that thunders.* He renamed them the Victoria Falls in honour of his Queen. His 1858 expedition up the River Zambezi and the ill fated use of a paddle steamer, the *Ma Robert*, imported from England in sections then built up, makes interesting but sad reading. The story of how he was 'lost' for months and 'discovered' by Stanley in 1871 is well known.

Less well recognised and remembered are how he had to trek without pack animals because of the indigenous tetse fly which wiped out cattle and all such, of his many days of hunger and thirst, his own severe and debilitating malaria and fever[12], his many encounters with wild men and wild beasts. Back in 1843 he was mauled by a lion which permanently damaged his arm. At such a time he wrote, "I'd rather be in the heart of Africa in the will of God than on the throne of England out of His will."

His converts were few, perhaps because he stayed so short a time in one place. He often preached with very few visible results. One convert, Sechele, a Kwena chief, was baptised in 1848 but did not show much progress - polygamy and other African customs were difficult to leave behind. But Livingstone's great

---

[11]For example *David Livingstone, Missionary and Explorer*, J Alfred Sharp, Epworh Press, 1929.

[12]He had 27 attacks of malaria fever during 3 years of travel, all the while searching in vain for malaria-free areas. He and many of his team used a quinine preparation called Livingstone Rouser pills which dramatically improved recovery.

legacy lies in how he influenced others and motivated mission work to this day especially in southern Africa. He had written, "I will place no value on anything I have, except in relation to the kingdom of Christ." He sowed widely and many others have entered into the harvest of his labours.

Last Long Journey

He started his last journey in August 1872 from Ujiji on the shore of Lake Tanganyika but soon became extremely ill with dysentery and fever. To compound the problem, his medicine chest was gone, stolen by one of his men who had deserted him. In January he was being carried across the Benguela swamps (in present day Zambia) by a few of his faithful men up to their necks in muddy water, often covering only 1½ miles a day.

At Chitambo's village, Ilala, near the head waters of the River Luapula he could go no farther. They built a hut for him, and on 1st May 1873 they found him kneeling by his bed, dead and still. He had written on his last birthday, his sixtieth, six weeks before, "My Jesus, my King, my life, my all, I again dedicate my whole self to Thee. Accept me, and grant, O gracious Father, that ere the year is done I may finish my work."

His death was probably due to cerebral malaria coupled with many intestinal complications. His heart was buried under a mvula tree at the place where he died. Jacob Wainwright, a freed African slave, read the burial service[13]. His body was dried and embalmed then carried 1,000 miles to the coast by two devoted Africans, Chuma and Susi, along with Wainwright. It was then shipped from Zanzibar to Southampton and arrived on the morning of 15th April 1874. Surrounded by vast crowds, on the quayside a small African boy held up a placard with the words 'TO THE MEMORY OF DR LIVINGSTONE, FRIEND OF

---

[13]Wainwright carved LIVINGSTON 4 MAY 1873 on the tree. It was cut down in 1899 and the inscribed section sent to the Royal Geographical Society in London. The site is now marked by a permanent memorial about 20 miles along a gravel road signposted off the main road between Serenje and Samfya in Zambia.

THE AFRICAN', while a 21-gun salute was fired at one minute intervals.

His body was identified by the mis-shapen arm bone resulting from the attack by the lion. He was buried with great pomp and ceremony in Westminster Abbey beside other great men of the Empire. Along the edge of his gravestone in brass lettering can still be read the text of John 10.16, the words which had motivated this outstanding life:

Other sheep I have, which are not of this Fold:
Them also I must bring, and they shall hear my Voice.

BC

CHAPTER 9

Mary Slessor (1848 – 1915)

In the 19th century, it was rare for unmarried women on their own to venture abroad from the shores of Britain, and almost unheard for single women to be accepted for foreign missions work in their own right. The women who did go were usually accompanying their husbands in their missionary callings as we have seen in some of our previous chapters. One of the very first single women from Britain to change this was Mary Slessor[14]. In 1876, at the age of 28 she left Dundee in Scotland to serve her Lord in an uncivilised place called Calabar in what is now Nigeria. What she faced when she arrived there, and how she courageously confronted wickedness, cruelty, debauchery, and lawlessness is an epic story worth reading[15]. This chapter can give only an outline of her remarkable life in the service of God and man.

Scottish Background

Mary Mitchell Slessor was born in Aberdeen on 2nd December

---

[14]Amy Carmichael went from Belfast to south India in 1895. From the USA, Charlotte White went to India in 1816, a freed slave called Betsey Stockton went to Hawaii in 1823, Cynthia Farrar went to India in 1827, Lottie and Edmonia Moon went to China in 1872-73. They mostly worked as teachers in mission schools, and sometimes in the wider community, and laid foundations which greatly benefitted others who followed them.

[15]An interesting and thoroughly researched account is Bruce McLennan's book, *Mary Slessor, a Life on the Altar for God*, 2014, Christian Focus Publications, Fearn, Scotland.
An older style fulsome biography is W P Livingstone's *Mary Slessor of Calabar*, 1st Edition 1915, 47th Edition 1940, Hodder & Stoughton, London.

1848, the second of seven children. Her father was Robert Slessor, a shoemaker to trade, but sad to say he became deeply addicted to drink and lost his job. When he suggested moving to the expanding industrial town of Dundee, his wife Mary agreed, hoping that his destructive habits would be left behind. So in 1859 they made their home in a single end tenement in the Cowgate, a crowded slum near the city's busy jute and linen mills. Robert became a labourer at one of the mills, but his drinking habits were not left behind, and meagre earnings quickly disappeared. The family was in dire straits many a day, with weekly visits to the pawn shop to see them through while trying to conceal the problem from others. Their youngest child Janie was born at this time, but three of their other children died, as did Robert himself shortly afterwards due to his tragic lifestyle.

Mrs Slessor was already working as a weaver, a 58 hour week for 10 shillings (50p), and when Mary was eleven she too went into Baxter's mill as a "half-timer". That meant 6am to 11am at the mill, then midday to 6pm at Baxter's new school where she obtained a very basic education. Her spiritual life was nourished more thoroughly by her own godly mother who took her family to the Wishart Memorial Church[16] in the Cowgate. Her conversion at the age of 12 was through the influence of an old widow who frequently gathered in the children from their play to tell them of the Saviour and the awful peril of hell fire if they did not repent and believe.

When Mary was 14 she became a full-time weaver alongside her mother. Soon she became the main source of income for the family as her mother's health was failing due to the many stresses she had to face. Mary had a great quest for knowledge which she developed at evening classes. She became a serious reader, getting to love the Bible, especially the Gospels, and also reading and distributing evangelical and missionary pamphlets. While still living in Aberdeen, Mrs Slessor had already nurtured

---

[16]George Wishart, Scottish martyr 1546; see *Torchbearers of the Truth*, Volume 1 in this series, p 40.

missionary awareness in her family's minds. When William Anderson from Calabar visited their church in Dundee, they heard moving accounts of that dark place in Africa. Mrs Slessor hoped that Mary's younger brother John would go there as a missionary, but sadly John was a weak and ailing lad. He emigrated from Scotland to New Zealand where he died shortly after landing.

While Mary earned the family income, she was no less committed to the work of her church. She taught in the Sabbath School and Bible Class, and in a nearby shop in the evenings she gathered in the many neglected and rough boys and girls from the streets to teach them from the Bible. One evening a particularly rough gang of boys waylaid her with the intention of breaking up her little mission. One of them swung a lead weight on a string nearer and nearer to her head to intimidate her, but even as it grazed her forehead she never flinched. Struck by her steadfast courage, they went in to the mission with her, and this lad later confessed that this was a turning point in his life[17].

During these 14 years or so in Dundee, Mary was being prepared for her future work. She began to think that she could maybe go to Calabar in place of her brother John. The social deprivation and slum conditions all around, the curse of strong drink, the squalor endured by large families, the unruly behaviour of gangs, the excesses of sinful behaviour – all these were moulding her thoughts and strengthening her character for the greater challenges she would face at Calabar.

To Calabar

In 1874, when Mary was 25, news of David Livingstone's death spread through Scotland. For many, including Mary, this was the catalyst for action, so in 1875 she offered herself to the Foreign Mission Board of the United Presbyterian Church. With

---

[17]A stained glass window in the McManus Galleries in Dundee portrays this incident along with later aspects of her life.

reluctance on the part of some but enthusiastic recommendations from others she was accepted, and in December of that year she went to Edinburgh for three months of intensive training. Alongside her heavy learning schedule she became involved in mission work in the slums of that city along with some other young women.

In August 1876 Mary Slessor set sail from Liverpool on the steamer *Ethiopia*. As she watched the ship being loaded with casks of spirits she said, "Scores of casks and only one missionary." She would soon see the havoc this trade was creating in Africa. After a month long voyage they reached the estuary of the Calabar river where a small boat ferried her to the shore at Duke Town to begin her life's work. Soon she would write home, "Oh, for a heart full of love to Jesus and to those perishing ones for His sake."

A mission at Calabar had been in existence for around 32 years. It had come into being through the desire of emancipated African slaves in Jamaica to take the Gospel back to their native continent. Around a million slaves had been shipped to the West Indies from Calabar itself in the previous 100 years, and that ignominious trade had led to petty chiefs at the coast becoming rich and important at the cost of countless lives of misery. Mary arrived to find an established and organised mission with a few simple buildings including a chapel, along with some trade in palm oil, but only a few miles up-river there were unexplored regions full of lawless and hostile tribes. The area was desperately unhealthy due to endemic African diseases and the unsanitary habits of the people. In fact the west coast of Africa had become known as the white man's grave[18].

Changes to make

In Duke Town, Mary worked first alongside others as a school teacher, but she did not really find it fulfilling. She wanted rather

[18]In 65 years, the Lyons Society for African Missions had prematurely lost 283 missionaries in West Africa.

to get out to pioneer on her own, and for that purpose quickly learned the local language. However, after just three years, she had to go home to Scotland because of malaria.

On her return, she was moved up river to Old Town where she was able to live as she wished, just like the local people. Human skulls were everywhere, stuck on poles or worshipped as totems. She learned about their customs and saw their evil practices, often feeling overwhelmed by the gravity of the tasks now facing her. But she gained the respect of the tribes-people even when she began to interfere with their horrible ways. One of these was the wicked habit of killing new born twins and the cruel ostracism of their mothers. She rescued many of these babies and early on adopted one little girl whom she called Janie after her own little sister.

After another three years, Mary was sent home again due to illness and she took Janie with her. For over three years she was able to look after her sick and ailing mother and sister, while travelling around to tell people about west Africa and the evil ways and customs of its people, with Janie being a graphic illustration. Soon after her return to Africa, her mother and sister both died. Upset and lonely she wrote, "There is no one to write and tell my stories and troubles and nonsense to." But she added, "Heaven is now nearer to me than Britain, and no one will be anxious about me if I go upcountry."

So it was that in 1888, Mary went farther into the interior, north to Okoyong, a dangerous area that had been hostile to others in the past. The farther she travelled, the greater were the evil habits she was confronted with. More human skulls were on display all around her. The men wanted only to get guns to be powerful, chains to keep their slaves, and liquor to dull their minds. They were frequently drunk and frenzied especially at palavers and funerals. When chiefs died their wives and slaves were killed "to accompany them into the afterlife". They had never heard the gospel, they respected only vengeance and cruelty, they did not know what love was. Mary brought to them the love of

Christ, trusting in God to show her how to change and win these savage people to Christ.

In these confrontations with lawless people and their cruel ways she believed that a woman would be less threatening than men. She wrote, "It seemed sometimes to be almost miraculous that hordes of drunken, passion-swayed men should give heed and chivalrous homage to a woman." For 15 years she stayed there teaching them, nursing them, and being a peacemaker. She rescued hundreds of twin babies thrown out to die, prevented many wars by personally coming between the warring factions (all the while knitting - sometimes for a whole day!), stopped the common practice of administering poison to determine an accused person's guilt. She often healed the sick, and told them all about God's great love in sending His Son to earth to die on the cross so that sinners might be saved.

Charles Morrison was a young missionary teacher in Duke Town. He fell in love with Mary, and although he was 18 years younger, she agreed to marry him, but only if he was willing to come to Okoyong. However he became ill and had to return home. Mary continued alone with her adopted children in a mud hut shared with large rats and tiny ants and other small jungle creatures, her lifestyle the most basic and frugal. She was not over-concerned about health precautions or cleanliness. Her clothes were of simplest style, not the petticoats and dresses worn by British women at the time. Her life was motivated by the love of God, and sustained by complete dependence upon Him through prayer. She wrote, "My life is one long, daily, hourly, record of answered prayer." Along with this, daily reading and meditation on God's Word moulded her character and supported her endeavours[19].

Still Onward

In 1903, now with seven children in her household, she moved

---

[19]One of her Bibles containing her own cryptic handwritten notes can also be seen in the McManus Galleries in Dundee.

on from Okoyong to do pioneer work in other even more remote areas such as Itu and the Azo, among a dreaded cannibal tribe. Her reputation as a great and wise woman and as a fair and honest judge had gone before her into that land. At first they showed little interest in her message, but soon many accepted Christ. Mary reported that in one town there were two hundred converts. None of them could read, so she pleaded for pastors to come to instruct these new Christians.

During this latter part of her life, Mary continued to do all she could. She walked the jungle paths until she was too old and feeble. Some Scottish friends sent her a cart that could be used to pull her around the villages. She prayed that God would give her the strength to finish her task among the cannibals, so she kept going. The respect she won among all these lawless, warlike tribes came to the attention of the British authorities, and eventually she was made an official judge and magistrate for the whole region. Official recognition embarrassed her, and she said, "I am Mary Mitchell Slessor, nothing more and nothing other than the unworthy, unprofitable, but most willing, servant of the King of Kings."

In 1915, after nearly 40 years in Africa, she died at the age of 66 in her own mud hut surrounded by her adopted girls. A government boat was sent to carry her body down the river to Duke Town, and she was buried on a hillside by the mission station to which she had first arrived. On the centenary of her death, a new memorial to her was erected in the centre of Dundee.

BC

CHAPTER 10

J Hudson Taylor (1832-1905)

In Chapter 5, some of the difficult pioneering evangelical work of Robert Morrison in China has been described. However, his work and influence were largely confined to the coast at Macau. Now half a century later, Hudson Taylor would expand that work much farther to reach into the interior of that vast country. His vision led eventually to the establishment of the China Inland Mission (CIM) and through it, the Gospel of the grace of God would reach many thousands who had never heard the name of Christ.

The CIM was founded in 1865, after Hudson Taylor had been in China from 1854 to 1861. In 1861 he had to return home for respite and recovery from illness, and it was then when he was in England that he had a deep experience with God in an intense struggle in prayer while alone on Brighton beach. Prayer would become the hallmark of his life from now on. He prayed for enough missionaries to send two into each of the twelve provinces of inland China.Thus in 1865 his family with sixteen others left the relative comfort of Britain for the hardships of China, eight more having preceded them. That was the start. Then in 1881, he prayed for another seventy missionaries, and seventy six went. In 1886 he prayed for a hundred within a year, and soon another one hundred and two were ready to go. Today, millions of Chinese believers are testimony to the sacrifices of these servants of God and of those who followed them, and to the abiding power of the Word of God in spite of the serious and often violent attempts during the 20th century to suppress and eradicate Christianity in that huge and now prosperous country.

From the start it was understood that all CIM personnel would depend entirely upon God for financial support. No income was guaranteed. Needs would only ever be made known to God in prayer. Hudson Taylor's life and service as well as his motivation and support were rooted in the power of prayer which he proved over and over again. He claimed the promise of John 14.13: "Whatsoever ye shall ask in my name, that will I do, that the Father may be glorified in the Son."

Early Life

James Hudson Taylor was born in the mining town of Barnsley in Yorkshire on 21st May 1832, into the family of James Taylor, a pharmacist and Methodist preacher, and Amelia (Hudson). In his early youth he rebelled against his Christian upbringing, until one day, going aimlessly into his father's study, he picked up a tract entitled *It is Finished.* It arrested his attention, and convicted of his sinfulness he was saved there and then. At that very hour, 80 miles away, his mother was agonising in prayer for his salvation. God answered.

His parents had a deep interest in mission work in China, and had been praying that their son would actually go there. This prayer too was answered when he announced in 1849 that this was to be his life's work. A contact with Edward Cronin who had been in Baghdad with Anthony Norris Groves encouraged him.

First he moved to Kingston upon Hull as a medical assistant, preparing himself for a life of faith and service. He lived frugally, preaching in the open air in the poorer parts of the town and distributing many gospel tracts, all the while studying Mandarin, Greek, Hebrew, and Latin in his spare time. He also proved God and the power of prayer several times while helping the poor. One night he gave away the last silver coin he had to a destitute widow to feed her children, leaving him with nothing. The next day he received a package containing a gold coin worth ten times more. He said, "That's good interest. Invested in God's bank for twelve hours and it brings me this!" When he was 20, he was baptised by Andrew Jukes in the assembly of believers in

Hull. He then studied medicine at the Royal London Hospital as further preparation for China. During this time he fellowshipped with the Christians who met in Brook Street Chapel, Tottenham.

To China's Hardships

He offered himself to the recently founded Chinese Evangelisation Society as their first missionary. Leaving Liverpool on 19th September 1853 on board the clipper *Dumfries,* he arrived in Shanghai 23 weeks later after a voyage which nearly ended in disaster.

In China, he found civil war raging. His first year was beset with difficulties. He started preaching and distributing tracts around Shanghai, but found out that he was being called a "black devil" because of the black overcoat he wore! So he adopted Chinese dress and the pigtail hairstyle which was common at that time. Many, including fellow missionaries criticized him for this. But he in turn believed it was not right for them to spend so much of their time as translators to businessmen and diplomats. His burden was to get the Gospel into the interior of China and so he set off along the Huangpu River distributing Bibles and tracts.

In 1857, the Society became unable to support its missionaries, so he resigned. A letter from George Müller at this critical time helped him to see that he could and should trust God for everything he needed. A little later all his medical supplies were destroyed in a fire, and on a journey inland he was robbed of nearly all he had.

He married Maria Dyer, daughter of missionaries in China, who was working at a school for girls in Ningbo. Their first baby died in 1858, but a daughter Grace was born a year later. They took over the work of the hospital in Ningbo when Dr. William Parker could not continue. The church there grew to 21 members, but by 1861, Hudson became seriously ill (probably with hepatitis) and it was then that he had to return to England to recover.

During the next five years in England he continued with Bible translation. He also completed his medical diploma and took a course in midwifery. He travelled extensively and wrote papers to promote more awareness of China's great needs. Four more children were born before all the family returned to China with sixteen new missionaries on 26th May 1866, on the tea clipper *Lammermuir*. Twice the ship was nearly wrecked, and they survived two typhoons, but at last they arrived in Shanghai on 30th September.

In a letter to his sister Amelia he had written, "If I had a thousand pounds China should have it - if I had a thousand lives, China should have them. No! Not China, but Christ. Can we do too much for Him? Can we do enough for such a precious Saviour?"

More Trials in China

Once back where his heart was, it was to an exhausting schedule of medical work and preaching every day. Hundreds came to hear and to be treated. In 1868 they travelled to Yangzhou to start a new work, but during a riot the mission premises were attacked, looted and burned. This led to outrage at home and some criticism of the CIM and of Taylor himself. Some members of the British Parliament called for the withdrawal of all missionaries from China. However, they continued steadfastly in Yangzhou and saw many more converts.

Another daughter, Maria, and a son Charles, were born, but then the older daughter Grace died of meningitis. This sad trial helped to bring more harmony within the diverse group of missionaries when they saw how Hudson Taylor placed the needs of his fellow workers above concern for his own daughter. In July 1870, baby Noel was born but he died of malnutrition. Worst of all, Mrs Taylor herself died from cholera several days later. Her death was the worst blow he had to endure. He became ill himself, and returned to England to recuperate.

He then married Jane ("Jennie") Faulding who had been with the CIM, and they returned to China in late 1872. In Nanjing, Jennie gave birth to stillborn twins. During the winter of 1874 he was back in England, after a fall on a Chinese river boat had nearly paralysed him. But when he was able, he preached throughout the country, profoundly influencing many including the famous cricketer C T Studd who was converted along with two of his brothers at that time. Studd was one of "The Cambridge Seven" who would go to China in 1885 (see next chapter).

Jennie remained in England with the children while he went back to China with more missionaries. The Chefoo Convention between Britain and China in September 1876 gave missionary work in China a legal status. So he was able to travel more freely and many mission stations were established. Jennie returned to China in 1878 and began promoting aspects of women's missionary service there. With so many to reach, Taylor arranged for unmarried women to go into the interior, something new which again had its critics!

He returned to England in 1883 and recruited more missionaries. Back in China there were now 225 missionaries and 59 churches, evidence of a greatly expanding work of God. Five years later he travelled to the United States, and 14 American missionaries joined them soon afterwards. He met Cyrus Scofield and D L Moody, both of whom became active supporters of the work of the CIM.

News of the dreadful Boxer Rebellion in 1900 and the resulting disruption of missionary work distressed Taylor greatly. The CIM suffered more than any other mission – 58 missionaries and 21 children were killed. But that only led to additional growth and further interest in missions in China.

By now Hudson Taylor was over 70 years old and his physical and mental health were failing. He was semi-retired, and went to Switzerland along with his wife. She died there of cancer in 1904. After that he returned to China for the eleventh and final time, visiting Yangzhou, Zhenjiang and other cities.

He died suddenly at his home in Changsha while he was reading. He was buried next to his first wife, Maria, in a cemetery at Zhenjiang near the Yangtze River. It was destroyed by the Red

Guards during the Cultural Revolution and industrial buildings were built over it. But his lasting memorial lies in the great heritage of the Christian missionary work which he pioneered, remaining effective far beyond his lifetime and far beyond the boundaries of China.

BC

Other details in www.wholesomewords.org/biography/biorptaylor.html: *J. Hudson Taylor: God's Mighty Man of Prayer.*

CHAPTER 11

Charles T Studd (1860-1931)

C T Studd, as he has become known, is remembered for several reasons which call for him to be included in this book.

- A brilliant young man, he turned his back on unique fame as a top class English cricketer to become a pioneer missionary in China, South India, and central Africa, a real trailblazer of the Gospel.

- Along with this, he relinquished an immense inherited fortune, and lived in the most basic and frugal way, wholly trusting in God to supply all he needed.

- He was one of the "Cambridge Seven" who left England for China in 1885.

- He was the founder of *Worldwide Evangelisation Crusade (WEC)* which continues its work in many countries today.

- He is the author of the memorable eight stanza poem with the refrain

  Only one life, 'twill soon be past; Only what's done for Christ will last.

- Many of his sayings are still widely quoted, e.g.,

  "If Jesus Christ be God and died for me, then no sacrifice can be too great for me to make for Him."

  "The light that shines farthest shines brightest nearest home."

> *"Some want to live within the sound of church or chapel bell;*
> *I want to run a rescue shop, within a yard of hell."*

The Studd Family

Mr Edward Studd made a fortune in 19th century India from indigo production, and returned to England to enjoy it, where he bought Tidworth Hall, a lavish stately mansion in Wiltshire. He immersed himself in social events and country sports like horse racing and fox hunting which he developed on his large estate. But when another country gentleman of his acquaintance coaxed him to come and hear D L Moody preaching in London, Edward Studd was soundly converted at the age of 57, and his life totally changed. All that mattered now was to see others saved, and he began with his own family. As it was, he lived only another two years to do this, and he did it earnestly and effectively.

His three sons were then at Eton, the famous public school, where they all excelled at cricket. They were not sure what had happened to their father when they were told about it, for their upbringing had been respectable but not evangelical or even religious. When home for their summer holiday to play more cricket, their father made it his business to question them about their souls' salvation and brought preachers to his house at weekends. During one of those weekends, all three were saved, Kynaston, George and Charles, although they did not tell their father or each other until they were back at Eton, bringing a joyful surprise to them all! Charles went up to Cambridge University to continue his studies, but his main interest was still cricket. He excelled so much in every aspect of the game that his career was described as "one long blaze of cricketing glory"[20]. His Christian faith however became lukewarm.

This changed dramatically when called to the bedside of his

---

[20]The famous cricket trophy, the Ashes, dates from 1882. On the urn is a short poem containing his name.

brother George who was critically ill, but miraculously recovered. Now he saw his life in the light of eternity. He went to hear Moody again and the joy of his salvation was restored to him, and along with this, a fervent desire to serve his Lord and Saviour. Cricket still beckoned, but his heart was no longer in it. He witnessed faithfully to other team members and Cambridge men, got some of them to go and hear Mr Moody, but in his heart he knew this was not enough. He thought, "How could I spend the best years of my life for the honours and pleasures of this world, while thousands of souls are perishing every day without having heard of Christ?" His motto-text was Mark 8.36. He had heard of the great unevangelised land of China and firmly resolved to go there, but his family, including his now widowed mother, did not approve. Along with this he was seeing many students being saved, but he believed he had received his marching orders for China.

The Cambridge Seven

After an interview with Hudson Taylor, now the director of the China Inland Mission (CIM, see previous chapter) Charles was accepted as an associate member. Very soon another six Cambridge graduates, most of them with eminent sporting or academic backgrounds, joined him to make up a band of seven, all of whom would go to China and would make lasting impressions in the sphere of Christian missions[21]. This was the answer to the specific and repeated prayer of Dr Harold Schofield, an earlier medical missionary with CIM who had gone to China at the age of 29. He reported that the province of Shansi had 9 million unsaved souls and only six missionaries, and his prayer was that God would send men from the universities at home as evangelists and Bible teachers.

The reputation of the seven spread rapidly. Such a move as theirs was unprecedented: brilliant, gifted, educated men abandoning

---

[21]See www.wholesomewords.org/missions/bcambridge7.html.
The seven were Stanley P. Smith, Dixon Hoste, William Cassels, Montague Beauchamp, Cecil Polhill-Turner, Arthur Polhill-Turner and Charles T. Studd.

their prospects of wealth and fame to go to a dangerous and backward foreign land to face a hazardous and uncertain future. Before they left England, they toured universities throughout England and Scotland where they spoke with great earnestness to capacity crowds of students. Their testimonies led to thousands of university men being saved of whom not a few would also take their place in making the Gospel known at home and abroad.

China

They sailed from England in February 1885 and arrived in Shanghai a month later. Their first task was to adopt Chinese dress and appearance, including pigtails, for the Chinese continued to be suspicious and wary of foreigners. Their first month in Shanghai was blessed with several conversions including that of the Chaplin of the Cathedral, but their objective lay inland, thousands of miles away. They worked hard at language study and quickly became fluent.

Three of them travelled first to Hanchung, 1800 miles by the Yangtse and Han rivers, which took three months, before continuing on foot for several weeks, covering up to 40 miles a day, to meet Hudson Taylor at Pingyang-fu. Then it was Studd on his own with native colporteurs, often barefooted because his sandals broke up, suffering blisters and cuts which somehow he was able to ignore. He lived and ate like the Chinese people, believing that this was the best way to reach them for Christ - life was hard although he never said so. Accommodation overnight was often denied them so they slept where they could and ate what they could find. Their testimony was that the Lord always provided just what they needed, for they needed so little.

He was now 25 years old, the age at which he was due to inherit his share of the family fortune. He believed he could not keep it and remain a true follower of Christ, so he began to give it all away. He sent £5,000 to D L Moody, another £5,000 to George Müller, and £15,000 to five other causes which he deemed worthy, including the Salvation Army's work in India. This left him with about £3,400 when the estate was wound up.

Two years later he fell in love with Priscilla Stewart, a young Ulster lady who was a missionary in Shanghai. First by correspondence, then together, they became convinced that they should get married, but not before each assured the other that Christ would always have first place in their affections. Their wedding was a simple one, first unofficially by a local pastor, then registered at Tientin by the Consul. They were married in their ordinary clothes to the consternation of many onlookers! Just before this, he gave his £3,400 to Priscilla for their future together. She said, "Charlie, what did the Lord tell the rich young man to do?" "Sell all." "Well then, we will start clear with the Lord at our wedding." And the money was given away for the Lord's work, most of it to General Booth who was told in the accompanying letter that it was from "your loving, we know, and getting humble, we trust, would-be soldiers of Jesus Christ".

As a couple they served the Lord in several towns in inland China, often separated from each other because workers were few. Both suffered frequently from fevers and malnutrition as they lived like those around them, each at different times being close to death's door. Their four little girls were born in China and a little boy who lived less than a day (later in England another baby boy died in infancy). Difficult births without experienced help and their little boy's death were severe trials which they bore uncomplainingly. Their funds were often at rock bottom, but after nights of prayer their need was supplied. Their practice was never to solicit funds from any source but to trust in their faithful God, whom they proved countless times in unexpected ways.

They saw many Chinese people converted and churches formed, although often being regarded with suspicion as "foreign devils" and having to move on, followed by curses and threats. Eventually after ten years in China, ill health caused them to return to England reluctantly. After a difficult journey with the four little girls to Shanghai, they sailed second class on a German steamer and made their home with Charles's mother in London in 1894.

India

During 1896-97, C T Studd now in better health was invited to visit some American universities because his brother, Kynaston, had already gone there with D L Moody to spread the story of the Cambridge Seven. Like their tour of Britain years before, Kynaston's visit similarly moved and motivated many American students, resulting in the formation of the Student Volunteer Movement which encouraged personal involvement in missionary work. When Charles visited and addressed thousands at scores of colleges, many more were truly converted and surrendered to the call of Christ to trust and follow Him.

Back in England, he remembered India, Tirhoot in fact, the place where his father had made his fortune. He felt a debt to take the Gospel to the indigo planters there, so in 1900 he went and spent six months among them. He was then asked to become pastor of an independent church in Ootacamund where he served for the next six years. Although suffering frequently from asthma, his ministry was greatly blessed not only among the planters but also among the soldiers, officers and government officials stationed there. Mrs Studd and their four girls enjoyed these years with him. All four girls were converted during that period, and baptised by their father in a large tub built into a flower bed in their garden just before they returned to England in 1906. Each of them came to love and follow their parents' Saviour.[22] Back home, the generosity of others provided for their education at some of the best private schools in answer to their parents' continual trust in the Lord to supply all they needed.

Africa

For the next three years, C T Studd became well known in many evangelical enterprises throughout England. In spite of poor

---

[22]The youngest daughter Pauline married Norman Grubb who became director of WEC after her father died. He wrote the excellent book which provided much of the information in this chapter, *CT Studd, Cricketer and Pioneer*, Lutterworth Press, 1933.

health, his plain speaking and forthright manner led to many a conversion in formal meetings and "chance" encounters.

One day in Liverpool he read a notice which said, "Cannibals want Missionaries". He saw the humour in it, but it became a serious call to action. He would go to central Africa, south of the Sudan, much of which had still not been reached by the Gospel. No one would back him up. Doctors said No – he was too sick a man, nor had he any funds. But convinced of the call of God he persevered and prepared to go, and on 15th December 1910 he sailed on his own to Port Said and thence travelled to Khartoum. He saw much blessing as he preached to British soldiers stationed there.

He trekked to southern Sudan, then took three months to get farther south through malaria infested country which caused his old illness to recur. From there he learned of masses of depraved and destitute Africans over the border in Belgian Congo who had never heard the Gospel. So during a brief return home, after writing eloquent pamphlets[23] and making stirring visits to Cambridge and elsewhere, the Heart of Africa Mission (HAM) was formed. It became the genesis of the Worldwide Evangelisation Crusade (WEC) which would reach far beyond Africa in its missions[24].

Parting from his wife again was very hard. Both felt it keenly, facing the likelihood of not seeing each other on earth again. In February 1913 he was sailing once more to Port Said, with only one companion, Alfred Buxton, fresh from a medical degree at Cambridge. These two, a worn out, gaunt old man and a fresh young man would soon be going with the Gospel into the heart of Belgian Congo, facing great dangers and overcoming countless barriers. In sincerity, realizing it was all God's work,

---

[23]These have been called the most stirring appeals in modern missionary literature, e.g., *The Shame of Christ, The Chocolate Soldier.*

[24]Up to CT's death in 1931, almost £150,000 had been provided for the work of WEC, around five times what he had given to God in China at the beginning.

CT nicknamed the two of them "Balaam's Ass and Noah's Dove"! On foot and by bicycle they travelled hundreds of miles until they reached Niangara in the very centre of Africa on 16th October 1913. The people they went to were completely uncivilized – every kind of evil was commonly practised and accepted.

Home for a short visit he sought more recruits, then in July 1916 he was on his way back along with his daughter Edith who would marry Alfred Buxton[25]. He had led the work in CT's absence, and on 19th June 1915 twelve had been baptized giving clear testimony to their repentance and salvation. The Gospel of Christ was changing cannibals, murderers, adulterers, thieves and drunkards to become children of God. But more was to follow in a mighty stream of truly converted Africans until we read of hundreds more coming to Christ and meeting in churches to learn of Him, while many of them would soon be taking the Gospel to their own people.

For the next 13 years C T Studd continued his life's work for his Lord from his home *Ibambi* in the Ituri forest. It was a simple structure with the most basic furnishings. He translated the New Testament and the Psalms into one of the native languages. He suffered several heart attacks at that time, nevertheless travelled away out west to the mouth of the River Congo, taking the great Gospel message to thousands more. One of his last meetings was in 1931 when a church was packed with around 600 men and 400 women all declaring their allegiance to Christ, willing to take the gospel to others. He preached on the Pearl of Great Price, but was too weak to stand.

All the while in England, Mrs Studd, although a helpless invalid previously, had become a tireless and effective secretary at the new mission headquarters in Upper Norwood, London. It was a sore blow to him when he heard of her death, only two years before he died himself on 16th July 1931 from a malarial fever with underlying causes due to gallstones.

---

[25]Their baby Susan was the first white one to be born in central Africa. Another of CT's grandchildren, Noel Grubb, died there too on his first birthday.

Around 2,000 Africans stood by as the frail, worn out body of the one they called *Bwana Mukubwa* was lowered into the soil of central Africa by a few white men. *Mukubwa* means big – not only in stature, but in thought and deed, in faith and love, in the knowledge of God and the Scriptures, in sacrifice and suffering for others, in ambition to take the Gospel into "regions beyond".

They sang,   *"Standing by the cross,*
We shall help each other,
Standing by the cross!"

BC

CHAPTER 12

Frederick W Baedeker (1823 – 1906)

The vast country of Russia has had a chequered history for as long as we can remember. Its people have endured much suffering - the harsh climate with extremely cold winters has always brought hardship, and much political upheaval has been the cause of countless deaths. In the early decades of the 20th century under Lenin and then Stalin, millions of peace loving citizens were uprooted from their homes and suffered terribly in the Gulags while an extreme form of communism was being enforced[26]. During World War II, Hitler broke his cynical August 1939 Non-Agression pact with Stalin by invading Russia. Its people subsequently suffered immense losses of life and property at the hands of the Nazis[27]. Since then there has been the Cold War, when the USSR and western powers built up huge nuclear arsenals to threaten one another, and Russia was a closed country to most foreigners, with all religious activity severely restricted within its borders. A few brave souls were able to enter parts of the country and encourage the believers who had "gone underground", to emerge years later and flourish in many places.

---

[26]Described by Aleksandr Solzhenitsyn (1918-2008) in *The Gulag Archipelago*, said to be one of the most influential books of the 20th century. He also said, "If I were asked today to formulate as concisely as possible the main cause of the ruinous revolution that swallowed up some 60 million of our people, I could not put it more accurately than to repeat: Men have forgotten God; that's why all this has happened."

[27]Over 20 million were killed, the highest number for any country involved in the war.

Before all this, when Russia was still being governed by the elite Czars, a choice servant of the Lord of German birth, Dr F W Baedeker, heard God's call to take the Gospel to its largely forgotten millions. He brought the Word of Life to members of the aristocracy to begin with, and then to many thousands of miserable prisoners in jails across that vast country. How he did this is an amazing story of dedication, perseverance and commitment to Christ and the Gospel which can only be outlined in this chapter.[28]

Dr Baedeker and the English Connection

Fritz Baedeker, as he was known at home, was the second youngest child of F W J Baedeker and his wife Frederika who lived at Witten in Westphalia. Father was somewhat detached from family life, an expert ornithologist, author of a beautifully illustrated book, *The Eggs of European Birds*. Mother was strict but fair in bringing up their six children.

When he was 16, Fritz was apprenticed to a business in Dortmund, then at 23 he enlisted with the German army for two years of military service in Cologne. During his short army career his health gave way and he was discharged, much to his delight. He obtained a PhD in Philosophy from the University of Freiburg, and he married a young lady, Auguste Jacobi in 1851 but sadly she died only three months afterwards.

Now began a period of travelling, first across Germany, then to London from where he set sail for Tasmania on a voyage beset by storms which took over 130 days. In Tasmania he became tutor in a private school, then moved to Melbourne and later to Sydney. In 1858 he returned to France, thence to his family for a short time, followed by a final move to England to settle and teach in a school in Weston-super-Mare, where he became a British subject. On 17th June 1862 he married a young widow,

---

[28]*Dr Baedeker and his Apostolic Work in Russia* by Robert S Latimer (1908, now out of print) is one of the few books which provide a more complete story - gratefully acknowledged for information used here.

Mrs Ormsby, the mother of a young boy at his school, and theirs became a long and happy marriage. They moved to Bristol to enable him to attend lectures on medicine and surgery for a year, and here he made a lasting friendship with another well known fellow-countryman, George Muller.

He was converted to Christ in 1866, then a man of 43. It happened in West-super-Mare at meetings conducted by Lord Radstock, arranged by the Earl of Cavan. Dr Baedeker reluctantly agreed to a friend's invitation to one of the meetings, became interested but kept himself remote until Lord Radstock reached him one evening and said, "My man, God has a message through me for you tonight." The two men were soon on their knees in an ante-room where he trusted Christ and the joy of salvation flooded his soul. Later he would say of this experience, "I went in a proud German infidel, and came out a humble, believing disciple of the Lord Jesus Christ. Praise God!" His wife held back at first, but seeing the great change in her husband went with him to a meeting where she too was saved, and became united with him in a desire to serve the Saviour they had found.

From England to Russia

For nearly 40 years Baedeker would be engaged in spreading the Gospel. For the first ten years he preached in his home area to good effect while he studied the Scriptures carefully. In 1874 Lord Radstock visited Berlin where an American evangelist was preaching the Gospel. On seeing the need for an interpreter, he called upon Dr Baedeker who passed on the message so enthusiastically that the German people said, "Here is a man of our own race and tongue upon whom the Holy Ghost manifestly rests. We will listen to him!" So he continued for a year and conducted his first Gospel campaign in his native land. Many were saved, among them several of the aristocracy, some of whom provided premises for the preaching of the Gospel for years to come.

It was Lord Radstock again who gave him an opening into Russia through his contacts with influential figures in St Petersburg.

Seeing great opportunities among a people largely deprived of the Gospel, he moved to Russia with his wife and daughter for three years, first to preach to its German-speaking people. But soon the field would open up until his ministry would cover much of what is now regarded as eastern Europe and extend subsequently to the western, northern, and southern provinces of the Russian empire as it was then. In St Petersburg, the Countess Princess Lieven provided him and others such as George Muller with a home from home as well as a place to preach.[29]

On arriving in a new city, he would approach its Governor and announce that he had come from England as an evangelist and ask whether he could hold a meeting in his drawing-room. Surprisingly to us, such a request was usually granted at once and in such luxurious surroundings in several cities he preached the Gospel to capacity crowds, and many were truly converted. His audience would often comprise people of many nationalities so that often he had to employ interpreters to translate his English or German into three or four other languages at the same time! Some of his hosts suffered for their involvement, such as Colonel Paschkoff, a wealthy officer of the Imperial Guards, who was banished from the country at the orders of Emperor Alexander III because he refused to give up using his palace for evangelism.

This method did not always work, however. Seeking permission through various layers of authority he would come up against a blockage – usually from the priest of the Orthodox Church which was powerful and influential. So he would sometimes proceed without official permission and continue until he was stopped. He spoke about 'hostile priests and active police' inhibiting progress in many places. On one occasion in Riga after he had arranged and advertised Christian Services he was forbidden because the police said that only the Orthodox Church could hold such Services. So he changed his title to "Lectures" which they

---

[29]The princess wrote the 'Introductory Note' to Latimer's biography of Baedeker in which she said, "He was much loved here. The simple brethren called him *dedouchka* (dear grandfather). Love to his Lord ever filled his heart."

could not forbid - the subject was "Sin and Salvation". Later on, religious freedom came and was granted officially in the 1905 Edict of Liberty of Conscience. That did not last, however, as the 20th century would later witness.

Into Prisons

While the value of Dr Baedeker's work among the Russian aristocracy cannot be underestimated, by stark contrast his greatest mission field was in jails across the continent where countless thousands of prisoners languished in the most appalling conditions, largely neglected and forgotten. How he travelled to reach them is an epic story in itself.

For 18 years he had free access to every prison across Russia, including frozen Siberia and the notorious penal settlement on Sakhalin Island. Through the influence of the Countess in St Petersburg he was able to obtain an official permit, renewed every two years, which gave him "special command to visit the prisoners of Russia, and to supply the convicts with copies of the Holy Scriptures". Such authority opened every prison to him, where he preached the Gospel and distributed thousands of copies of the New Testament supplied by the British and Foreign Bible Society. These were transported in cases to where he was going next by special arrangement of the authorities.

Conditions in the prisons were dreadful. Overcrowding, filth, vermin, lack of sanitation, along with cruelty from prison guards combined to make convicts' lives a complete misery. With heads half shaved, usually shackled by the ankles, they were forced to march long distances from one prison to another. There most would exist in despair until disease or brutality ended their existence. Most piteously, wives and children would try to accompany their men into exile, adding to the awful picture of destitution. Baedeker reported from Tobolsk that every week, 600 to 800 prisoners were coming in to its prisons, with 300 to 400 being sent farther east. One prison held 3,400 prisoners in sixteen wooden sheds. Many would make a vain attempt to escape, soon to starve and perish in the cold.

In places such as these Dr Baedeker brought hope and cheer with his kindly attitude and comforting words from the Scriptures. Hardened criminals and political prisoners alike (including many Christians and others incarcerated for their religious beliefs) were often reduced to tears, but uplifted and grateful to receive New Testaments. Some requested their visitor to write his name on the books "so that they would remember to pray for him". Prison Governors too appreciated his visits and his concerns, for many of them also deplored the conditions in which they worked, and longed to see improvements made. These would eventually happen, in some measure due to Baedeker's influence.

The Long Journey

From St Petersburg on the Gulf of Finland across to Russia's eastern coast on the Pacific is a distance of over 5,000 miles. Dr Baedeker first made this epic journey between March and October 1890 at 67 years of age. It began in Berlin, on to St Petersburg and Moscow by train, and then by steamboat on the River Volga to Perm. 500 poverty stricken emigrants accompanied him on the ship, and moved by their plight he provided a hot meal for them. Another train journey took him across the Ural Mountains into western Siberia, then several days on another steamboat on the River Obi took him to Tomsk. At each stopping place he made it his business to visit the prisons and leave tracts and New Testaments which had been shipped ahead for his arrival.

The next thousand miles or so were by road, at least such roads as existed. The mode of travel was by *tarantass* which can best be described as a primitive type of covered wagon pulled by three horses. His cases of books were packed in first, then luggage on top, some food supplies, and finally a mattress and pillows for such comfort as could be had travelling over uneven roads, mud flats and through rivers. They covered about 120 miles a day, the fast horses changed at various stations en route. The countryside they passed through was beautiful in springtime, but days were hot and nights very cold necessitating many layers of fur clothing.

The tarantass was conveyed by boat across Lake Baikal, to travel another 1,000 miles through Siberia to Stretensk. Siberia was the destination for political exiles and the most hardened criminals to be given hard labour in the silver mines in arduous conditions. He wrote home to say that during his long journey he had preached the Gospel to 40,000 prisoners and distributed 12,000 copies of the Word of God.

The final leg of the journey was 1,800 miles by steamer on the River Amoor to the coast and then to Sakhalin Island, a place even more desolate and cruel than much of Siberia. At this final stopping place, he continued his task with unabated zeal for the benefit of thousands of others living in hopeless despair. His return homewards was via Tokyo on 23rd September, then Shanghai, Hong Kong, Singapore, Colombo, and Port Said, finally arriving in England in early December.

He testified to the goodness of God during the whole of that long, arduous journey across Russia. He had been preserved from attacks by the many brigands lying in wait by the way, had always been provided with means of transport although basic and comfortless, and with suitable clothing for the extreme cold. In spite of many visits to the most unsanitary and unhealthy places, he never contracted any serious disease.

Dr Baedeker's work continued for many more years. He made a second journey across Russia like the first. He laboured for some years in Finland, Sweden and Norway. There it was numerous prison visits again, but also meetings in some universities brought blessing to professors and their students. In Armenia, and notably where the River Volga[30] enters the Caspian Sea, he spent some time with believers he met, and continued unabated his prison ministries there and in the Caucasus although he suffered frequent bouts of fever at that time. He also made a visit to Canada to minister to a community of Germans of whom he had heard.

---

[30]Part of his earlier epic journey across Russia had been on the upper reaches of this same river.

His home base was in Weston-super-Mare where his wife patiently waited for him, wrote to him, and always welcomed him back. He enjoyed fellowship with the believers in the Gospel Hall in Waterloo Street and his contributions to their work and worship were memorable. He often preached in the open air to crowds of holidaymakers on the sands.

Dr Baedeker died after a short illness and his body was buried in Weston cemetery. Lord Radstock preached a fitting tribute and farewell to crowds in the Gospel Hall and at the grave. Mrs Baedeker had the following inscription put on his headstone, to include words frequently on his lips during his last few days:

FRIEDRICH WILHELM BAEDEKER, Ph.D.

WENT IN TO SEE THE KING IN HIS BEAUTY,

SAVED BY THE PRECIOUS BLOOD OF THE LORD JESUS,

OCTOBER 9TH, 1906.

AGED 83 YEARS

BC

CHAPTER 13

John Williams (1796 – 1839)

When Christopher Columbus sailed westward across the Atlantic his purpose was to pioneer a route to China and the East Indies. Instead a new Continent was discovered. Soon after the discovery of this New World, the Spanish conquistadores realised that another ocean, lying beyond the Americas, would have to be traversed in order to reach the East. How wide that ocean was none could tell until the survivors of the voyage led by Ferdinand Magellan[31] had returned to Spain in 1522. Only then did Europeans gain some sense of the real vastness of the Pacific.

Over 50 years later Sir Francis Drake led the first English circumnavigation westward round Cape Horn, across the Pacific and Indian oceans, and home via the Cape of Good Hope. There was further exploration during the 17th century, however the greatest discoveries in the Pacific Ocean were made during Captain James Cook's three voyages between 1768 and 1779. Cook was not only a consummate seaman but a highly skilled navigator, surveyor and cartographer. He accurately mapped the east coast of Australia, New Zealand and many Pacific islands.

The increased knowledge of the South Seas led to contact and trade with the indigenous people in the widely scattered island groups. One sad consequence of this was that before long many of them began to suffer the ravages of alcohol and contagious disease. This is not to imply either that all Europeans

---

[31]Magellan was killed in the Philippines, but one ship returned to Seville in Spain thus completing the first circumnavigation of the globe.

were exploitative or that life previously had been idyllic. The Polynesians had spread eastwards to colonise the islands in the huge sea area bounded by Hawaii, Easter Island and New Zealand successfully voyaging over the trackless ocean in large sailing canoes. Yet they were heathen, and practised such horrid activities as human sacrifice and cannibalism.

The beginning of South Sea Missions

As knowledge of such savagery and cruelty filtered back to Europe many earnest Christians became burdened to take the Gospel to them. One such was Thomas Haweis who made an abortive attempt to send two missionaries on board a Royal Naval vessel voyaging to the Pacific in 1791[32]. Disappointment did not dampen Haweis' interest and he was active in the formation of the London Missionary Society in 1795. Perhaps it was due to his influence that Tahiti became the first field of labour of that Society's missionaries.

The preparation of a missionary

John Williams was born in Tottenham, then a country village 6 miles north of London, on 27th June 1796. His father was a descendent of one of two brothers, who in the reign of James 1 had been banished from Wales because of their nonconformity. He was taught by his godly mother until he left home to be apprenticed to a Mr Tonkin, an ironmonger in London. John was energetic and soon showed remarkable ability in metal working and in the practical knowledge of his trade. Like many another youth he tried to shake off the godly influence of home, yet God had His eye upon him.

One Sunday evening, 3rd January 1814, he stood near a street corner on the City Road London. Church bells were ringing, but an evening of pleasure with friends at the Highbury Tea Gardens had been planned. Providentially his friends were late and as John waited impatiently a lady passed by. It was Mrs Tonkin, his

---

[32] *Torchbearers of the Truth* Ch 26.

employer's wife on her way to the Whitefield Tabernacle. She invited John to come and after at first refusing he yielded and went with her. He heard preaching on Mark 8. 36-37 "For what shall it profit a man, if he shall gain the whole world, and lose his own soul? Or what shall a man give in exchange for his soul?" It was the turning point of his life and he left the chapel a converted man.

There was an immediate and radical change in his life. He sought opportunities for Christian service, and attended a class for young men preparing to enter the Ministry. One autumn evening in 1815 the class was informed of the conversion of Pomare, the King of Tahiti, and many of his subjects. An appeal was made for helpers and John William's heart was moved. He hid his desire until he felt himself definitely called of God. He was advised to apply to the London Missionary Society which he did in July 1816 and was accepted. On 3rd September, with eight companions including Robert Moffat[33], he was solemnly set apart for missionary service.

On 29th October he married Mary Chauner, who had prayed that she "might be sent to the heathen to tell them of the love of Christ". Within three weeks they sailed on the *Harriet* bound for Sydney. The ship called at Rio de Janeiro and at length reached her destination on 2nd May 1817. Williams had used the time wisely by closely studying the vessel and gaining much invaluable practical knowledge. Then it was on to Tahiti which they sighted on 16th November, before landing on Eimeo, a nearby island where a mission station had already been established.

The practical and the spiritual

Williams lost no time in applying himself to his vocation. He commenced language study and made rapid progress, being able to preach in Tahitian within ten months. His first sermon was from the text "This is a faithful saying and worthy of all acceptation, that Christ Jesus came into the world to save sinners". Another task he quickly tackled was boatbuilding. A

---

[33]See Chapter 7

vessel had been laid down three years before but lay unfinished. He undertook the iron work using material from an old anchor chain, and with hard work the small vessel was soon complete and named *Haweis*. New opportunities came when chiefs from nearby islands asked for teachers for their people. The Williams and two other couples responded and soon a good work was going on in Huahine and Raiatea.

This was the first step in a remarkable spread of the Gospel to the Society, Hervey, Cook and Samoan Islands in the south west Pacific. Among a noble band of workers, Williams emerged as an outstanding leader who made a lasting mark for God throughout Polynesia. His range of talents and personality were suited to the conditions. He had clear vision, boundless energy and total consecration. When native teachers and helpers were appointed to mission stations he counselled them, "Work well and pray much. Think of the death of Jesus, and reflect that the natives of the islands to which you go are purchased with His blood". He admired the words *Try* and *Trust* and said, "You know not what you *can* or *cannot* effect until you try; and if you make your trials in the exercise of *trust* in God, mountains of imaginary difficulty will vanish as you approach them, and facilities will be afforded which you never anticipated".

Tamatoa the king of Raiatea had recently been converted and many of his people wanted to hear the Gospel. By May 1820 a chapel had been erected and the first baptism had taken place. At that service 70 persons professed faith in Christ. Opposition was not lacking, and became violent with an attempt to murder Mr Williams. Four ringleaders were sentenced to death, but spared at the intervention of the missionaries. In 1821 Mr Williams baptised nearly 500 persons and the converts were united into a Christian church on Congregational principles. Children were now taught Scripture and examined thereon, where once infanticide had been widely practised, sometimes with incredible cruelty. One old chieftain said, "Oh that I had known that the Gospel was coming! Oh that I had known that these blessings were in store for us! Then I should have saved my children. I shall die childless although I have been the father of nineteen children".

Perils on land and sea

In the primitive conditions missionaries suffered from malaria and other tropical fevers and Williams and his wife fell seriously ill that year. They took passages in the ship *Westmoreland* which touched at Raiatea bound for Sydney. The rest and the change enabled both to regain their health. A schooner of 80 tons was purchased and named *The Endeavour* to be used for the furtherance of the Gospel and trade. Loaded with useful goods she sailed from Sydney on 23rd April 1822 and reached Raiatea on 6th June.

Mr Williams must have been deeply disappointed when he was censured by the Society's directors for purchasing *The Endeavour,* however he complied with their wishes and the schooner was sailed to Sydney and sold. This was not before some very useful work had been done in reaching various Hervey Group islands. In July 1823 Messrs Williams and Bourne sailed from Raiatea bound for Aitutai where two native teachers had been since 1821. They found the work progressing and that idolatry and cannibalism had been abandoned. This was most encouraging and Williams wrote in his journal, "I hope for great things, pray for great things, and confidently expect great things to result from these labours". On Aitutai he found natives of Rarotonga who were taken on board *The Endeavour* and brought to their home island. A faithful and courageous native worker named Papeiha volunteered to remain at Rarotonga where the work began in dangerous circumstances yet ultimately prospered.

Mr and Mrs Williams later returned to Rarotonga with Mr and Mrs Pitman who had been appointed to labour there. There was no harbour suitable for the ship to enter so the missionaries and their wives had to be put ashore in a boat. As Mr Williams was handing down his son into the boat he fell into the sea, and was only rescued from being crushed against side of the ship by the prompt action of Mr Pitman who pulled him with the boy into the boat. It was not a life for the faint-hearted!

Mr Williams had intended to stay on Rarotonga for only three months, but that became an extended period of isolation during which he was thrown back upon his own resources, and upon the Lord. This beautiful island was not fertile, and the missionary families suffered hardship. They had no European food of any kind, and local foods were not congenial. Months passed without a ship calling and Mr Williams became anxious about the believers in Raiatea, and concerned about islands not yet visited with the Gospel. He resolved to construct a boat and the result was a feat of ingenuity - not only in building but also in fashioning the necessary tools and implements. A successful trial voyage of *The Messenger of Peace* (approx. 60 ft.) was made to Aitutaki about 170 miles distant. This small schooner did amazing work and proved to be capable of lengthy voyages. In April 1828 the Williams returned in her to Raiatea. She was then used to make visits to various island mission stations to strengthen and consolidate the Christians. Translation of Scripture in Tahitian had already been undertaken by earlier missionaries and now on top of all his other work Williams translated some New Testament books into the Rarotongan language. Charles Pitman and Aaron Buzzacott translated other books and Mr Buzzacott saw to the printing of the New Testament. It was a difficult task because the limited vocabulary of the language had first to be produced in a written form.

In 1830 he set sail on *Messenger of Peace* bound for the Samoan Islands, 1,500 miles eastwards, visiting other islands on the way. The seed sown yielded a bounteous harvest. A second voyage was made to Samoa two years later, when after departing Rarotonga the schooner made an excellent run of 800 miles in only five days. Christian witness was consolidated at Upolu on Savaii, the largest island of the Group.

The Williams decided to visit England and arrived there in June 1834 almost 18 years since they had left as very young missionaries. His reports aroused great interest as did his book *Missionary Enterprises in the South Seas.* Mr Williams was convinced that a ship was needed to progress the work and he appealed to Christians to contribute to the cost of purchasing and converting one. There was a generous response and more than sufficient funds were soon raised. A brig[34] named *Camden* was bought, and on 11th April 1838 John and Mary Williams boarded it. They had decided that their younger son Samuel should remain in England. It was a sore parting and the lad would never see his father again. Sixteen new missionaries were on board and each day they were taught the Tahitian and Rarotongan languages. It was an uneventful voyage to Sydney and on to Upolu Samoa where the Williams made their home. From here visits were made to Rarotonga and other islands.

Premonitions

On 3rd November 1839 John Williams embarked on *Camden* to make a long wished for visit to the New Hebrides island group, now called Vanuatu. Some of the natives were known to be fierce and hostile and Mary urged caution on her husband, indeed entreating him not to land on Erromanga. In his last sermon at Upolu he referred to Acts 20.37-38, "and they all wept sore, and fell upon Paul's neck, and kissed him, sorrowing most of all for the words which he spake, that they should see his face no more".

The first island visited was Fatuna where they found the natives friendly. On 19th November *Camden* lay off Erromanga and the following morning a boat was lowered under the charge of Captain Morgan to take Messrs Williams, Cunningham and Harris to the shore. On reaching shore they were given cocoanuts and some children were present. The three men then left the boat and walked along the beach until they reached a stream of water. Mr Harris then walked inland towards the bush where a number of natives with savage yells attacked him with clubs and spears. He ran back, but fell and was struck down. Mr Cunningham managed to reach the boat, but Mr Williams running to the beach with one native in pursuit fell into the water. Soon others joined the attack and the party in the boat

---

[34]A square rigged vessel with two masts

became helpless and horrified spectators to the tragedy as the missionaries were killed and their bodies stripped and dragged into the bush.

Captain Morgan sailed to Sydney with the terrible news. The Governor of New South Wales sent HM sloop *Favourite* to Erromanga to attempt to recover remains. They reached the island on 1st February 1840. The natives confessed that they had eaten the bodies. *Favourite* then sailed for Samoa, and on 24th March Mary Williams learned that she was a widow. She returned to England in 1845 and settled at Islington working as a tract distributor and visitor among the poor until her death in 1851.

Further attempts to evangelise Erromanga also had tragic results. In 1857 a Nova Scotian couple Mr and Mrs Gordon settled on the island. Initially they were well received but when a measles epidemic broke out they were blamed, and on 20th May 1861 both were brutally murdered. With amazing courage Mr Gordon's brother took up his murdered relative's work but on 7th March 1872 he too was killed by a native whose child had died.

There is however a happier postscript. In 2009 descendants of John Williams were invited to Erromanga to a ceremony in which they received an apology from those whose ancestors had killed and eaten the martyred missionaries. Mr Charles Milner-Williams and 17 other family members were present.

Converted natives deeply mourned the loss of John Williams who had been both an evangelist and a father to them. His death was a massive blow to his colleagues, but it was the crowning sacrifice to years of service. He had known the risks of his pioneering work, yet he persevered because of his compassion for lost souls. Years before he had written to his parents, "Grieve not at my absence, for I am engaged in the best of services, for the best of masters, and on the best of terms".

JB

Information in this chapter abstracted from the biography *John Williams of the South Sea Islands* by James J Ellis is gratefully acknowledged.

CHAPTER 14

James Chalmers (1841 – 1901)

The design and building of sailing ships in Britain reached its zenith during the 1850s and 60s, with Aberdeen shipyards at the forefront of developments. Many fast and lovely ships slipped into the water at the mouth of the river Dee, and in 1868 the famous tea clipper *Thermopylae,* the great rival of *Cutty Sark,* was launched. Three years previously, Alexander Hall & Sons, Aberdeen had received an unusual order. Their Yard Number 243 was built to the order of the London Missionary Society and named *John Williams.* She was a wooden three masted barque[35], 132 ft. in length and of 296 gross tons, the second of five vessels to bear the name of the hero of our previous chapter. On 4th January 1866 *John Williams* left London bound for Australia and the South Seas. Among the missionaries on board was a young couple, very recently married, and eager to begin their service for the Lord. Their names were James and Jane Chalmers.

James Chalmers was born in 1841 in Ardrishaig a lovely village on the western shore of Loch Fyne in the west of Scotland. When he was an infant his parents moved to Inveraray, just over 20 miles further up Loch Fyne, where he grew up and received his schooling. Although his parents were members of the Church of Scotland, James attended the United Presbyterian Sunday School. One Sunday the minister, Gilbert Meikle, spoke to the boys about mission work in the Fiji Islands and remarked, "I

---

[35]Square rigged on the fore and main masts, and fore and aft on the mizzen.

wonder if there is any lad here who will yet become a missionary, who will go to the heathen and to savages and tell them of God and His love". James was touched, and on his way home he knelt behind a stone wall and vowed to serve Christ. It was a fleeting impression, his vow soon forgotten and another event had to take place before that dormant seed could spring to life.

Conversion and call

Towards the end of 1859 two men from the north of Ireland came to Inveraray to preach the Gospel. The whole town was moved and James Chalmers, by this time employed as a solicitor's clerk, was brought under conviction. He had been neglecting Church services, but now anxious he confided in Mr Meikle who had a great interest in the young man. After a Sunday evening service he found peace in believing on the Lord Jesus Christ. The reality of his salvation was soon evident, as he joined the United Presbyterian Church, became a Sunday School teacher and engaged in Gospel work in and around the town becoming the means of awakening many to their need of salvation.

His next step was to work with the Glasgow City Mission. While in Glasgow he met George Turner, on furlough from labouring in Samoa, who spoke to him about the South Seas work of the London Missionary Society. Memories were stirred of Gilbert Meikle's appeal, and as James Chalmers pondered his future the way seemed to open for him to apply to the Society's Directors. He was accepted, sent to Cheshunt College for training, and in due course was appointed to serve at Rarotonga.

On 8th November 1865 James married Jane Hercus. Jane had experienced the gracious influence of a Christian home, and had been converted in 1858 while caring for her widowed grandmother in Kirkwall in the Orkney Islands. After her grandmother's death she returned to Greenock, and then moved with her family to Glasgow. When her family emigrated from Scotland to New Zealand in 1865 she went to Inveraray until her marriage in November. Behind Jane's meek and quiet spirit lay an indomitable resolve to help her husband in his missionary work.

An eventful voyage

January gales in the English Channel ensured a rough start to the voyage and *John Williams* had to put into Weymouth for repairs. After this the barque made a good passage to Adelaide and to other Australian ports, before sailing on to various Pacific Islands. It was not until 5th September 1866 that the vessel arrived at Aneityum in the New Hebrides, and while entering the harbour struck a submerged reef. Three days of strenuous efforts succeeded in bringing her off the reef, but the ship was leaking badly forcing a passage to Sydney for repairs. *John Williams* returned to Aneityum and went on to call at other islands including Niue where she arrived on 8th January 1867.

This island is surrounded by a coral reef and goods and people could only be put ashore by boat. It was a dangerous location, and in the afternoon sail was set and the barque stood off the land for safety during the night. In the evening the breeze fell away and *John Williams* lay becalmed. A strong current then swept her back towards the island, and though her boats were lowered in an attempt to tow her to safety it was to no avail. That night *John Williams* crashed onto the reef and was wrecked, her career over all too soon. Mercifully no lives were lost, but it was a weary wait of three months before the Chalmers could leave Niue and continue their journey to Rarotonga.

Serving the Lord in Rarotonga

On 20th May 1867, seventeen months after leaving London, they reached Rarotonga, their hazardous journey now over. They found the people in some distress, as the island had been devastated by severe tropical cyclones in both March 1866 and March 1867. The new missionaries could do little to help as almost all their possessions had been lost in the wreck. They settled into the Mission House, so glad to be at last in their home and at their work. Another generation had grown up since the pioneering days of Williams, Pitman and Buzzacott, yet Chalmers felt that the best church members were among the old men who had been acquainted with the disgusting practices of heathendom and "remembered the rock from whence they were hewn". Traits of heathendom persisted with some, and he found that many were less mature in their faith than he had expected.

He also found that some young men were distilling alcohol from fruit juices to supply drunken orgies at secret places in the bush. This often led to serious fighting much to his great anxiety as he saw in it the ruin of many lives. Energetically and willingly he would tramp through dense bush in search of these gatherings where he spoke to the youths. They never insulted or were hostile to him, and some were turned from their evil ways. 1870 brought some revival to Rarotonga and good numbers of careless souls were converted. Many who had been excommunicated repented, and were restored, giving fresh impetus to the life and testimony of the church.

He made weekly visits to each of the village churches to teach the Christians and to preach the Gospel. His pastoral work aimed to raise the believers to a higher spiritual level with emphasis upon holiness and uprightness of life. An Institution for educating and training native teachers had previously been established, and Mr Chalmers took classes for two hours each morning for these young men. Mrs Chalmers taught their wives in a room at the Mission House. Many of these students became teachers and helpers to missionaries in places yet untouched by the Gospel. He tried to impress upon the people that they should become self-reliant, rather than dependent on European missionaries.

At first James and Jane felt their isolation. In two years they saw only one white Christian, and it was a joy when a replacement *John Williams* arrived. It enabled visits to be made to other islands of the Hervey Group. Some were fertile, but on others the people were very poor, subsisting only on fish and cocoanuts. In these poorer islands the Chalmers distributed clothing and other useful items sent by friends in Britain and Australia.

In May 1877 ten years of fruitful service on Rarotonga came to an end when with great sadness the islanders bade farewell to the missionary couple whom they had grown to love and trust.

James and Jane Chalmers had heard a call they could not ignore, and went to serve God in scenes and circumstances right at the cutting edge.

Pioneering in New Guinea

New Guinea, the world's second largest island, lies to the north of Australia. A range of mountains, stretching in an east west direction, has a number of peaks over 15,000 ft. with equatorial glaciers. There are rain forests, and some the world's largest mangrove forests, on both the northern and southern lowlands. The indigenous people are mostly of Melanesian descent, but their linguistic diversity is the greatest in the world. Over 1000 languages are spoken. European sailors had first sighted New Guinea in the 16th century, however few incursions were made by Europeans until the 19th century. The first visitors found it to be a dangerous place. Natives were hostile to foreigners, and fierce inter-tribal fighting with bows and arrows, spears and clubs was common as was head hunting and cannibalism. The people were animistic, believing spirits inhabited almost everything, and worshiped idols and the spirits of ancestors.

The activity of the London Missionary Society in New Guinea began in June 1871 when a small fact finding group led by Samuel Macfarlane landed at Hood Point on the south east coast. From the beginning the Society's missionaries were assisted by Polynesian teachers and pastors who made a significant contribution to pioneer evangelism in very hazardous conditions. An island in the Torres Straits beyond the northern tip of Queensland was initially used as a base, but by 1873 a mission had begun in the newly established Port Moresby[36] where William Lawes became the first permanent white resident in New Guinea.

James and Jane Chalmers arrived there on the mission schooner *Bertha* in October 1877. The intention was to extend the work

---

[36]This town became the capital of the British Protectorate of South East Papua New Guinea established in 1884. It is the capital of present day Papua New Guinea.

eastwards and on their first trip a suitable site was found on Suau Island, just off the coast, where houses for missionaries and teachers were erected. In April 1878 James, whose native name was Tamaté, began the first of many exploratory journeys in New Guinea. Mrs Chalmers accompanied him, in the small mission steamer *Ellengowan* which had been donated to the Society. In 90 of the villages the people had never before seen a white man. Some trips were made inland and on one of these Mr Chalmers narrowly escaped with his life. Great tact and courage were needed to conciliate the savage and suspicious people, but advances were gradually made.

The climate took its toll on Mrs Chalmers's health and she became so ill that James took her to Cooktown Queensland, from where she went on by steamer to Sydney. She was cared for by friends, but repeated fevers had so weakened her that she died on 20th February 1879. A message had been sent to call her husband, but he was not able to reach Sydney until 24th March. Two months later he returned to New Guinea and made his base in Port Moresby.

During the next year he led a party to explore the country and search for sites suitable for mission stations. They covered over 500 miles in the longest inland journey yet undertaken. At the beginning of 1881 the first three New Guinea converts were baptised at Port Moresby. One of these, named Aruatera, proved to be a faithful man in speaking to his own people of the Lord Jesus and His love. In March the first two women converts were baptised, but later in the month news came from Hood Bay, east of Port Moresby, that teachers and their wives and children had been massacred. A single spear slew both mother and infant in the case of each of the teachers' wives. Altogether twelve persons were murdered. This was a severe test coming in the wake of encouragements.

Mr Chalmers turned his attention westwards, and *Ellengowan* was used to go along the coast of the Gulf of New Guinea. At various stops he procured canoes to go up rivers to visit villages and tell the people why he had come to them. This was slow and painstaking work but natives were being brought out of gross darkness to be enlightened by the glorious Gospel of Christ and gradually the mission was extended. In 1886 good progress was made along the coast, new Rarotongan teachers arrived, and at many stations new converts awaited baptism.

In August of that year Mr Chalmers returned to Britain after an absence of over 20 years. While on furlough he wrote *Pioneering in New Guinea* for publication by the Religious Tract Society. New happiness came in his engagement to marry Mrs Eliza Harrison who, when Miss Large, had been a close friend of the first Mrs Chalmers. He returned to Port Moresby in June 1887 and after Mrs Harrison arrived the next year they were married on 6th October. In 1890 Chalmers revisited the Fly River[37] estuary, and adjacent coasts on the western side of the Gulf of Guinea. His travels pioneered, as he loved to, and consolidated the work. He visited Polynesian teachers at their outposts to cheer and counsel them. He was a strong man, now well used to the climate, but the strain would sometimes tell, and he suffered severe bouts of malarial fever. It was said that "the mosquitos are the real cannibals of New Guinea".

The last years

Mrs Chalmers' health deteriorated, necessitating her return to England in 1892. Mr Chalmers came home in 1895 for the London Missionary Society's centenary celebrations but returned alone to New Guinea in November, as poor health prevented Mrs Chalmers return until June 1897. She was a woman of strong character and deep missionary interest, so it was a grievous loss to her husband when she died on a Mission vessel not far from Daru Island near the mouth of the Fly River on 25th October 1900. She was buried on the island and tragically her husband did not long survive her.

---

[37]Named after the corvette HMS *Fly* used in a survey of the area in 1845. The river is 650 miles long, navigable for a considerable length and has a wide delta with many islands.

He had been joined, and much encouraged, by a young missionary Oliver Tomkins, who wrote of his mentor, "St Paul could not have been more considerate to Timothy than Tamaté is to me". In April 1901 Chalmers and Tomkins visited Goaribari Island north east of the Fly River, where the natives were known to be particularly ferocious. The two missionaries and some helpers went ashore from the Mission vessel. They were invited into the village longhouse, but after entering, the two white men were struck from behind with stone clubs and felled to the ground. They were immediately beheaded, and the others likewise killed. Their heads became trophies, and their bodies given to the women to cook, and to be eaten by these savage cannibals on the same day.

It was a terrible end, but God who had hitherto preserved them had allowed the fatal blows to fall. Friends and colleagues were shocked by the brutal murders. For James Chalmers it was the culmination of 23 years of consecrated service. He was called the Livingstone of New Guinea, a great pioneer missionary, explorer, preacher and teacher. Oliver Tomkins and the young helpers had been cruelly cut down in the dew of youth, yet their sacrifice was not less noble.

JB

Information in this chapter abstracted from the biography *James Chalmers of New Guinea* by William Robson is gratefully acknowledged.

CHAPTER 15

Lilias Trotter (1853 – 1928)

In October 1876 a genteel Englishwoman called Isabella Trotter and her daughter Lilias arrived at the Grand Hotel in Venice. On their journey Lilias had enjoyed sketching and painting the magnificent scenery of Switzerland and the Italian lakes. The famous art critic John Ruskin was also in the hotel and Lilias's mother wrote him a short letter with some of her daughter's watercolours requesting his opinion. He immediately recognised her potential and found her to be an able and teachable student. She was thrilled by his brilliance and his affinity with the natural world. Their meeting in Venice began a long friendship, but one by which Lilias was brought to a crisis point in her life.

A Christian family

Lilias's father Alexander Trotter had been a successful stockbroker, a strong character of high principles, with a personal Christian faith, who with his wife aligned with the evangelical party within the Church of England. Their family lived "the happy, disciplined life of the Victorian upper classes; godly, serious, kind to the poor at a distance, sheltered from all that was offensive. So Lilias grew, beloved and loving, in the sheltered atmosphere of a stable home, surrounded by beauty and culture"[38]. But in 1864 Alexander fell ill and two years later he died. This bereavement deeply impacted upon his sensitive daughter just as she entered adolescence, and her family recognised a change in her. It seemed that the loss of an earthly father had turned her towards

---

[38]*Until The Day Breaks* by Patricia St. John, OM Publishing 1990

her heavenly Father and often they would discover that Lily, as they knew her, had gone to her room to pray.

Spiritual influences

Two formative experiences came some years later. The first was the Broadlands Conference held in 1874 in the stately home[39] of the Rt. Hon. William Cowper-Temple. This conference was a precursor of the annual Keswick Conventions. Lily, now 21 years old was invited with her mother. The teaching[40] focussed upon practical theology and holy living and deepened her understanding of Christian faith and practice. It directed her to an inner life of surrender to God. The second experience in the first London campaign of D L Moody which commenced in March 1875 encouraged her to an outward life of serving God. Lily was already involved in Christian work connected with Lord Radstock, and Lady Kinnaird, who became a joint founder of the Young Women's Christian Association[41] (YWCA). She became a member of the team who counselled anxious souls after Moody's preaching. This experience formed in her a lifelong desire to bring souls to Christ. She never forgot Mr Moody's advice. "You must ply them with the Word of God. Work patiently until you see that they have grasped the truth, and are resting on Christ alone for salvation. Don't be in a hurry; think, oh think, what it means to win a soul for Christ and do not grudge time spent on one person."

The fork in the road

Lily was already committed to Christian work when she met John Ruskin. As he mentored her, he became more than ever convinced she had a unique gift. While Lily's artistic nature

---

[39]*Broadlands* in Hampshire later became the home of Earl Mountbatten of Burma through his marriage to Edwina Ashley.

[40]One of the speakers was Andrew Jukes who had resigned his Church of England curacy, submitted to believer's baptism and associated with brethren in Hull. He wrote a number of books including *The Law of the Offerings*.

[41]Lord Shaftesbury was its first president.

and talent blossomed under his tutelage, she did not forsake her responsibilities at the Welbeck Street Institute, a YWCA London hostel. She was balancing two aspects of her life, but becoming conscious that a choice would have to be made. It was Ruskin who brought matters to a head when he put before Lily the brilliant future he believed she could have if she gave herself wholly to the development of her art. It was an enticing prospect for a young woman of 26, yet her decision set her on an altogether different course. She wrote to a friend, "I see as clear as daylight now, I cannot give myself to painting in the way he means and continue still to seek first the Kingdom of God and His righteousness."

The friendship with Ruskin endured and in the closing months of his life in July 1899, she sent to him *Hymns of Tersteegen* writing "It has been full of light and blessedness to me and I have such a feeling that it will have some rays for you that I can't help sending it".

Working with the YWCA

Lily continued as secretary at Welbeck Street with fresh vigour. Her work was varied and became full time. She had responsibility for teaching, and her approach and methods were explained in *History Lessons for Junior Classes* published in 1884 by the Church of England Sunday School Institute. She provided a comprehensive presentation of Bible themes tracing "God's promise of the Day Dawn" from the creation in Genesis to the new creation in Revelation.

A dark underside of life in Victorian London was prostitution. Lily moved with compassion for the young women caught up in this vicious trade, went to extraordinary lengths to find and rescue "lost sheep" in the streets around Victoria Station. She brought many to the hostel to safety, a good's night's sleep and the possibility of being trained for employment. All were sure to hear of the compassion and love of the Good Shepherd. Other activities led to expansion into the larger Morley Halls.

Eventually the strain of unremitting labour took its toll. In 1884 she had surgery, which in her exhausted state left her seriously ill, forcing her to give up work for a period of convalescence. It was the first occurrence of a repeated pattern throughout her life of periods of overwork, followed by necessary rest and recuperation.

A missionary calling

In February 1885 the Cambridge Seven sailed from England to serve the Lord in China[42]. Their speaking engagements at the universities and widespread reporting stimulated fresh interest in overseas missions. Around that time the YWCA set up a foreign missions department but initially this seemed "altogether beyond the horizon" to Lily who again was busy with her work in London. She was stirred however when in May 1887 a three day missionary programme was arranged at Morley Halls. The speaker on the third evening was Edward Glenny, who only a few years earlier had been instrumental in beginning Christian work among the Kabyle people in Algeria. Lily sensed that God was speaking to her through Mr Glenny, and before another morning there remained no shadow of doubt that Algeria was in His plan for her.

On 14th July, her thirty-fourth birthday she applied to join the North African Mission but failed to pass their health examination, probably because of her weakened heart. She resolved to go independently with an understanding that she would "work in harmony with this mission but not connected with it". She left the leadership at Morley Halls to receive training at Mildmay Hospital. On 5th March 1888 Lily and Lucy Lewis left Waterloo Station with the chorus *Crown Him Lord of all*, ringing in their ears. They were joined at Southampton by Blanche Haworth for the sailing to France, then onwards by train to Marseilles, and finally by steamer to Algiers arriving on the evening of 9th March. They disembarked the following day, three women all of whom

---

[42]See chapter 11.

had health issues, who knew little about the country, and not a single word of Arabic, to begin a work with no one to guide or to advise. This was the small beginning of the Algiers Mission Band.

Christianity in North Africa

Some African countries are mentioned in the Bible. For example devout men from Egypt and the parts of Libya about Cyrene (Acts 2.10) were at Jerusalem on the day of Pentecost, and those who "gladly received the Word and were baptised", probably included Cyrenians (see Acts 11.20; 13.1). During the following centuries the Gospel spread along the North African coast, and many churches were established. Two famous 'church fathers' belonged to the region, Tertullian, born in 160 in Carthage[43], and Augustine, author of *Confessions* and *The City of God*, born in Numidia[44].

With the 7th century Arab invasion, Islam came in like a scourge. Christianity, at least in nominal form, survived in Egypt but not to the west. Some of the Berber people resisted forced conversions, and small Christian communities may have survived until the 12th century, but thereafter not a vestige remained, and for over 1,000 years dominant and intolerant Islam permeated every aspect of life and culture. In 1830 French forces captured the city of Algiers, deposed its Muslim ruler, and proceeded to subdue and colonise the country. With the influx of Europeans, churches were established in Algiers and other coastal towns, but native Algerians were entirely untouched, and strongly resistant to any Christian influence. Such was the country to which Lily and her companions had come.

First years in Algiers

Initially they lodged at the Pension Anglo Suisse until they could rent a flat in the French part of the town. There they began to study Arabic using the only study resource available,

---

[43]Near to modern Tunis.

[44]Part of modern Algeria.

a French/Arabic dictionary. Later they found a professional tutor, and prevailed upon him to translate portions of Scripture into colloquial Arabic. They printed copies on their typograph and went out into the old Arab town or Casbah with one of their few sentences, "Canst thou read?" They distributed their hand printed French and Arabic text cards in the public squares, and openings for conversation sometimes gave opportunity to practise their Arabic. Other initiatives were door to door visitation, and French speaking meetings in their flat which were so well attended that soon a larger place became essential. Progress in the first two years was painstakingly slow in the face of many obstacles. The often oppressive climate forced Lucy Lewis to return to England, but a start, however tentative, had been made.

In October 1890 Lily and Blanche returned to Algiers after a four month break in England and were joined by Helen Freeman. The three women made an indomitable team, ready to face difficulty and resistance. Each served the Lord in Algeria to the end of their lives. Improving fluency in Arabic enabled them to have weekly classes for Arab boys. Talking to street urchins in the Casbah opened doors to some homes. The life duty of an Arab woman was to serve men. She was the slave of her father from birth, and then became the slave of her husband till death. The women listened to the messages and even assented to some degree, but without real understanding. Jesus was held to be a great prophet but second to Mohammed. When Jesus Christ was presented as *the* way to God the response was "Jesus *and* Mohammed". Ahmed the first convert was baptised by another missionary Mr Lambert in April 1891, but days later he appeared at their home covered in blood after being attacked by 18 Arab men. It brought home the cost of following Christ in an Islamic society.

Growth of the work

The arrival of others, freed Lily and Blanche to make a first journey inland to Biskra. They walked from house to house, offering some basic medical services, and telling the people of the Lord Jesus. Word quickly spread about these strange European women. Responses were mixed. Some were interested, others resisted. Once their words were met with a chorus, "Mohammed is the one who saves us." After six weeks they returned by another route, visiting places where Gospels were received gladly by folk to whom a new book was a rarity.

Other journeys penetrated further south. Lily loved the desert. "Looking on and on, the desert stretched away like a great sea, broken only by an island of palms here and there. I shall never forget the sight of it. But the sense of rest and silence that lies in the immensity of it grows day by day." From the vantage point of a camel's back the artist's eye observed the changing contours of massive sand dunes and the patterns of light and shadow in the afternoon sun. She loved sleeping in a tent under the stars, but more, she loved the desert people and the privilege of telling them of the Saviour. For this she and Blanche and Helen endured the baking heat, the desert storms and many other discomforts, and the dangers too.

To deepen their contact with local Arabs they wanted to live in the Casbah. They leased a rambling old house and moved there in 1893. Neighbours were astonished that Europeans, who normally separated themselves from Arabs, were choosing to live among them in the native quarter, considered by most to be a slum. For many years this house served well as a base for local activities such as classes for children, and for ventures further afield. Lily and her colleagues were encouraged by each conversion and held a small weekly meeting to teach the few believers. Ramadan was always a great test for the converts, who were under enormous pressure to observe this annual fast. The missionaries and the converts were engaged in a spiritual battle, and felt the oppressiveness of the powers of darkness. Their recourse was persistent prayer. Muslim efforts to coerce Christian converts were both evil and subtle, sometimes using drugs, mixed unnoticed with food or drink, to excite the emotions and paralyse the will power, or using spells and enchantments.

Adding to their problems the French colonial government viewed Protestant mission work with suspicion. Tensions between Britain and France in the late 1890s worsened matters and for a period the work of the Algiers Mission Band was almost brought to a standstill. Happily French workers were available to help until the two countries reached better terms.

Slowly the number of workers increased, and the work expanded. The first outpost was established in 1900 in Blida a small mountain village 30 miles inland. By 1913, 25 years after Lily's and Blanche's arrival in Algiers, the Band had 25 members and nine permanent outposts. In 1906 an additional home in El Biar near Algiers was acquired. It would prove to be a haven for the three 'seniors'. They named the house *Dar Naama,* Arabic for "House of Grace".

Christians from two ships that called at Algiers in 1907 visited the house in the Casbah. One lady recorded her impressions, being greeted by a national believer with "a smile of joy that gladdened our hearts" and the "wee class of tiny children in an inner class room, a few benches, a small organ, a Bible picture roll, a very few helps for teaching". She saw a scroll stretched upon the inside wall of the court, marked into squares, indicating the millions in Algeria who had never heard of Jesus, and the small proportion of Arabic speaking missionaries. It powerfully showed the need for labourers.

Closing years

The First World War brought restrictions in travel and supplies, but opportunities arose to produce literature suited to Arab readers. In February 1918 Blanche Haworth fell ill with fever. At first it did not seem serious but she deteriorated, until on the morning of the thirtieth anniversary of their arrival in Algiers she passed quietly into the Lord's presence.

For another 10 years Lily, and Helen, continued to lead the Algiers Mission Band. Increasing physical weakness did not lessen Lily's cheerful outlook, and younger missionaries benefited from her experience and wisdom. From September 1924 she was confined to bed at *Dar Naama.* She continued to write and was able to complete *The Sevenfold Secret* a study of the seven "I Ams" of John's Gospel written especially for Sufi Muslim mystics. Another fruit of her life's evening was *Between the Desert and the Sea,* describing Algeria in poetic language illustrated by colour plates of her watercolours.

On 27th August 1928 Helen Freeman and other members of the Band were gathered in Lily's room. They sang her favourite hymn, *Jesus Lover of My Soul.* She stretched out her arms as though she would embrace them all then slowly lifted her hands in prayer. Almost immediately she became unconscious and in perfect calm she drew her last breath and went Home[45].

JB

---

[45]Page 324, *A Passion for the Impossible* by Miriam Huffman Rockness, Discovery House Publishers. The information abstracted for this chapter is gratefully acknowledged.

CHAPTER 16

Pioneers in South America

The great Trans-Atlantic voyages of Spain and Portugal, and their discovery of the New World at the turn of the 15th and 16th centuries had lasting consequences in South America. In a relatively short space of time Spaniards had conquered both the Aztecs and the Incas, soon establishing a colonial empire stretching from Mexico, through Central and South America, to Tierra del Fuego in the remote south. Portugal's colony began on the east coast and spread over that vast territory that is now Brazil.

The explorers and conquerors were followed by the Jesuits, so that Roman Catholicism became entrenched over almost all of the settled parts of South America. During the 300 years of that colonial era there was no opportunity for Protestant missionary activity. This began to change in the revolutionary period that followed the end of the Napoleonic wars, and was helped by immigration from Britain and Europe. By the end of that period nine republics had emerged from Spain's South American possessions. Generally the republican constitutions ensured religious liberty, however for many years the extent to which it could be enjoyed depended upon the strength of the local Catholic hierarchy's influence. It is not surprising therefore that the progress of Gospel work was slow and patchy through much of the 19th century. Yet over time many South American countries have become fields of significant missionary endeavour, where the Word of the Lord has had free course and has been glorified (2 Thess 3.1).

In 1805 the ship on which Henry Martyn voyaged from England to India called at Salvador on the Brazilian coast[46]. When he saw the large slave population and the outward signs of formal religion, like Paul in Athens, his spirit was stirred in him. Before leaving he stood at a vantage point overlooking the beautiful bay of All Saints and exclaimed, "What happy missionary will be sent to bear the name of Christ to these western regions? When will this beautiful country be delivered from idolatry and spurious Christianity? Crosses there are in abundance, but when will the doctrine of the cross be held up?"[47] Not too many years afterwards these questions began to be answered.

In the vanguard of the pioneers who brought the Gospel to South America are three men whose names may be largely forgotten, but whose lives and labours deserve our attention.

James Thompson (1788 – 1854)

James Thompson was born in Creetown, a small seaport on Wigtown Bay in south west Scotland. He may have been converted when James Haldane[48] visited the town, for after he had studied medicine in Edinburgh, and theology in Glasgow, he assisted Haldane in the pastorate of the Leith Walk Tabernacle. In 1818 he went to Argentina in conjunction with the British and Foreign Bible Society (BFBS).

The Tabernacle congregation paid for his passage and financed his first year. His prime objective was the promotion and distribution of Bibles but he also initiated public education in Argentina, and successively in Chile and in Peru. This earned him the respect of liberal Catholic but anti-clerical politicians, and he was granted honorary citizenship by the governments of these three countries. Thus the way was opened for other colporteurs

---

[46]Ch 3, this book.

[47]*Henry Martyn Saint and Scholar: First Modern Missionary to the Mohammedans* by George Smith. See also *That the World May Know*, Vol 2, *Dawn over Latin America* by F A Tatford, p128.

[48]*Torchbearers of the Truth* Ch 28.

to follow him. In Buenos Aries he commenced regular meetings and a Sunday School in connection with the small Baptist congregation that had been formed. This was just four years after independence, and prior to Argentina's constitutional law granting liberty of worship being ratified in 1825. He encouraged Bible translation into the Quechua and Aymara languages which at that time were spoken by many more people, and across a wider geographical area, than now. Quechua was spoken in the Andes areas of Peru, Ecuador and Bolivia, Aymara in regions to the south.

He went on to visit Brazil, Ecuador, Colombia and Venezuela, and later did similar work for the BFBS in Mexico and British North America, encouraging translations of Scripture into native languages[49]. The breadth of his work in an era when travel was difficult is amazing.

By his efforts to improve literacy and to make Bibles available, both in Spanish and indigenous languages, James (Diego) Thompson paved the way for evangelism wherever he laboured. This invaluable service places South American evangelicals greatly in his debt.

Allen Francis Gardiner (1794 – 1851)

Allen Gardiner was born at Basildon in Berkshire and brought up by parents who prayed for him. He was an adventurous youth and entered Royal Naval service as a volunteer in 1810. Early impressions faded but were never wholly lost though he began to regard reading the Bible as a waste of time.

One evening in an inn he overheard a father reading Scripture to his son, and though he almost interrupted good manners prevailed. Through that incident God spoke to him. He reflected on his upbringing, and resolved again to read the Bible. Over the next two years his earlier impressions deepened as he

---

[49]Information gratefully acknowledged from www.jamesdiegothomson.com and *An Evangelical Saga* (Ch. 4) https://books.google.co.uk

approached what became the turning point in his life. While he was serving on HMS *Dauntless* the vessel called at Tahiti, where he witnessed the remarkable results of missionary work. What he saw on Tahiti, and neighbouring islands, led to him resigning his commission in order that he might serve God.

He did not regard himself as a missionary, but rather as a pioneer opening a way for others. That may explain why, instead of focussing his efforts, he moved so widely. Nevertheless Gardiner endured discomfort and peril, and hazarded his life to accomplish what he believed God wished him to do.

Following a period in South Africa he went with his wife and children to Rio de Janeiro and from there to Buenos Aires. In 1838 he travelled across the pampas and over the Andes to Santiago and Concepcion on the Pacific coast. There he left his family to go on to Indian territory on the Chilean frontier. After a hazardous journey, crossing swollen rivers and such like, he found that the Indians, influenced by a Roman Catholic friar, were suspicious and hostile. He saw no likelihood of gaining a permanent footing there and rejoined his family at Concepcion. He faced similar problems on the island of Chileo where again he was unable to penetrate Indian communities.

Captain Gardiner hoped that in the extreme south he might experience less Catholic opposition, and succeed in reaching heathen tribes. In 1843 he made his first visit to the Magellan Strait on a small chartered schooner sailing from the Falkland Islands. The natives he met on Tierra del Fuego were marauding savages, but those on the Patagonian shore seemed to be more receptive to visitors. He then returned to Argentina and distributed large numbers of Bibles and tracts with no opposition from the civil government.

His burden to evangelise Patagonia and Tierra del Fuego remained, and he visited England to gain support. This led to the formation of the Patagonian Mission, later named the South American Missionary Society. Establishing a shore mission station seemed impractical, so two launches *Pioneer* and *Speedwell* were purchased. In September 1850 seven men, including three Cornish fishermen, sailed from England on board *Ocean Queen*. In December they arrived at Picton Island off the coast of Tierra del Fuego, not far to the north of Cape Horn. The enterprise lurched from one disaster to another in the bleak and inhospitable surroundings. *Pioneer* was driven ashore and wrecked in a gale. Their main stock of powder had inadvertently been left on *Ocean Queen,* leaving them with scant means of securing food. The natives were menacing, sickness soon appeared, and the first death occurred in the depth of winter about the end of June 1851. Another two of the party died in August, and on 4th September Gardiner made his final diary entry. The previous day he had written, "I am by His abounding grace, kept in perfect peace, refreshed by a sense of my Saviour's love", and "I commend my body and soul to His care, and earnestly pray that He will take my dear wife and children under the shadow of His wings".

The British Admiralty ordered a ship bound for the Pacific to search for the missing missionaries. The site of the tragedy was discovered, and the unburied remains interred with dignity.

When the tragic news of the deaths of the party became known, support for the Mission poured in. A schooner named *Allen Gardiner* was built and two later vessels also bore his name. The Mission expanded and his son, Allen Gardiner Jr later laboured in Chile[50].

Leonard Strong (1797 – 1874)

Leonard Strong's story brings us to British Guiana (now Guyana) on the north east of South America. The climate and the terrain of the country lying about 3 to 8 degrees north of the equator could not be more different from that of Tierra del Fuego. The British, Dutch and French Guianas were the only parts of South America

---

[50]Information gratefully acknowledged from *Life of Captain Allen Gardiner*, http:// anglicanhistory.org

not colonised by the Spanish or Portuguese. British planters had developed sugarcane and cotton production in the colony and brought slaves from Africa to labour on their plantations.

John Wray of the London Missionary Society had arrived in Demerara in 1808 and pioneered with the Gospel. He preached, and taught slaves to read. A congregation was established in a chapel built by a planter with an interest in the wellbeing of his slaves. All this roused much opposition and the colonial authority intended to expel Wray, who then sent a petition home signed by supporters of his work. The Society appealed to William Wilberforce, who took up the cause with Lord Castlereagh with the result that Wray was allowed to remain in the colony.

In 1817 John Smith was sent out by the Society. A slave rebellion broke out on plantations on the Demerara River in 1823 and Smith was falsely accused of inciting rebellion and concealing his knowledge of it. He was arrested, tried and sentenced to death. A petition was submitted to the House of Commons against the sentence, but while waiting a pardon, Smith died in his cell in the common jail. He had been in ill health, and the conditions in the jail hastened his end[51]. The ensuing House of Commons debate about the scandal became influential in the abolition of slavery in the British Dominions. These turbulent events were in the very recent past when Leonard Strong arrived in British Guiana early in 1827.

He was the second son of Robert Strong, a Church of England rector at Brampton Abbotts in Herefordshire. At an even younger age than Allen Gardiner he joined the Royal Navy as a midshipman, and saw a good deal of action in the 1812-14 war with America. While serving in the West Indies he had a narrow escape from drowning when his boat capsized in a squall and he was awakened to his need of salvation. He left the Navy and was admitted to Magdalen Hall Oxford to study

---

[51]Details concerning Wray and Smith can be found in the digitised version of *The History of the London Missionary Society 1795-1995* Chs XIV and XV.

with a view to ordination. It may have been while at Oxford that he was converted.

While still an undergraduate Leonard offered himself for service with the Church Missionary Society. His College Principal recommended that he should first complete his studies under his father's guidance which he did and was ordained in May 1826. Initially he had thought of going to New Zealand but this changed following his romantic interest in a young lady named Frances Reed whose father owned a plantation at Demerara. Mr Reed's son managed the plantation and desired the services of a clergyman in his area. A revised plan was approved by the CMS committee and Leonard and Frances were married in November 1826. They left for Demerara the following month.

Leonard Strong had an independent mind, and notwithstanding the attitudes of many planters he burned with zeal to preach the Gospel to the slaves. The CMS committee were pleased to learn that he had been licensed to officiate in St Mary's parish in Demerara and thus had opportunity "for promoting the spiritual profit of the slave population". It was not long however until the anger of planters grew to the point that he was forced to move to Georgetown, where he became rector of St Matthew's in 1830. He had had serious questions about the liturgy and the Prayer Book, and his induction as rector required his assent to things which he no longer believed to be Scriptural. This troubled his conscience until in 1837 he resigned his position at considerable financial loss. He began to preach in a shed to large numbers of now freed slaves. God blessed his labours, and soon Christians were meeting to take the Lord's Supper in the simple manner practised in New Testament times[52].

In 1842 George Muller heard of this remarkable work and began

---

[52]This date is taken from *Leonard Strong: the Motives and Experiences of Early Missionary Work in British Guiana* by T C F Stunt. Others have written that Strong's secession from the Church of England took place in 1827 but Mr Stunt's research proves the later date to be accurate.

to support Mr Strong through the Scripture Knowledge Institution which he and his colleague Henry Craik had founded in Bristol in 1834. In 1840 John Meyer from Switzerland arrived in the colony. He had been studying in London at the CMS Institute but left in 1839. Before returning to Switzerland he attended meetings of an assembly in London where one evening he heard a letter from Leonard Strong read out. Meyer felt guided to that field of service, and he took the Gospel to the Arawaki Indians in the interior. His service was relatively short as he took malaria and died in 1847, but a work had been established and others continued it.

Leonard Strong had a furlough in England in 1843 and when he returned a Mr and Mrs Barrington accompanied him. He finally returned to home in 1849, and settled at Torquay where his ministry became greatly appreciated. He passed away in 1874.

JB

CHAPTER 17

Into Brazil and Venezuela

Brazil has been called the Portuguese Colossus. This huge country covers nearly half of South America stretching from 5 degrees north of the equator to almost 34 degrees south. For a long time the Amazonian rain forest remained largely impenetrable and other regions were thinly populated. Immigration however changed this during the 19th century and the ensuing development of the country brought opportunities for Gospel work.

Beginnings in Brazil

The British and Foreign Bible Society activity initiated by James Thompson (previous chapter) was probably the earliest evangelical work but it was not until mid-century that Protestant missionary work began in earnest. Two Presbyterian missionaries came to Rio de Janeiro around 1859. Their work led to the remarkable conversion in 1864 of a Roman Catholic priest, Jose Manuel da Conceicao[53], who left the Church and devoted himself to itinerant evangelism. He visited scattered towns and villages with only his Bible and a small medicine wallet to minister to both spiritual and physical needs. He often encountered violent opposition and worn out by sufferings and privations he died on Christmas Day 1873.

Richard Holden, a native of Dundee, had worked in Brazil as a

---

[53] *That the World May Know* Vol 2, *Dawn Over Latin America* p 131; www.theopedia. com/jose-manuel-da-conceicao.

merchant and had learned Portuguese. He studied theology in America returning to Brazil in 1865 as a cleric and missionary. In 1872 he withdrew from the Anglican Church and began to meet in the name of the Lord Jesus alone with around 30 other believers in Rio de Janeiro. This small assembly gathered in the house of a brother named John Menezes. Mr Holden also helped a small group of believers in the State of Rio who had been converted through the work of colporteurs. Later he moved to Portugal and died in Lisbon in 1886.

Stuart Edmund McNair (1867 – 1959)

Stuart McNair was born in Brighton but grew up in Croydon, the second oldest of nine children. His parents had been members of the Church of England, but may have withdrawn from its communion as Stuart later recounted that when 14 years old he attended a Bible Reading in Croydon led by John N Darby[54] who took time to shake his hand. He went on to qualify as a civil engineer and when his employment took him to Dublin he was regularly invited to the home of C H Mackintosh. On one occasion McNair confided to his host that he believed the Lord was calling him to serve Him in South America. Mr Mackintosh put his hands upon his head and prayed for God's blessing on his service[55].

In 1891 McNair took up employment in Lisbon where he lodged with Richard Holden's widow and her son. His time there was good preparation for his service in Brazil where he arrived in May 1896. He laboured first in and around Rio de Janeiro. A family named Belo had been converted through the work of BFBS colporteurs in Rio. This family moved out into rural parts where settlers were clearing the forests to prepare the land for farming. The sons were ardent in the Gospel, and around the town of Carangola, in Minas Gerais[56], a good number were saved. Stuart

---

[54]This would have been in the last year of JND's life.

[55]*Some Reminiscences* by Stuart McNair 1954; *The Life and Times of Charles Henry Mackintosh* by Edwin Cross.

[56]A large inland State to the north of Rio de Janeiro.

McNair was able to visit these new believers and teach them from the Scriptures. He travelled elsewhere, to Pernambuco and Belem in the north, and also made visits to Argentina and the Falkland Islands.

In 1905 he returned to Portugal to evangelise among students at Coimbra University. He seems to have thought that his service in Brazil was over until he received a letter from a Syrian believer who had immigrated to the State of Maranhao in Northern Brazil. Miguel Matter insisted on McNair coming and paid his fare so he responded to this call and spent a happy and fruitful time there.

In 1913 he travelled south to Carangola. He found that Manuel Belo's preaching had been blessed, and that at a farmhouse at Conceicao do Carangola 50 believers were breaking bread[57]. In six other places in the area congregations were functioning as local churches. Challenged by the need for Bible teaching McNair settled in the region. He started a night school to teach believers to read and study the scriptures. In 1917 he visited Harold St John in Argentina[58] and asked him to consider coming to help in a 'Bible school' at Carangola. Mr St John was very interested and came to look more closely into the matter. The two men visited every little Christian gathering within a radius of 50 miles from Carangola, and after St John saw the hunger and thirst for teaching he returned to Argentina to bring his wife and children to Brazil. After their day's work in the fields about twelve young men studied from 5 - 8 pm. Reading, writing, and other subjects were taught by McNair, and the Bible by St John. When Charlotte McNair joined her brother in 1919 she started classes on baby care for Christian mothers. The 'Bible school' sessions continued until Harold St John left Brazil in 1921 and were of lasting practical and spiritual value to simple believers living in primitive conditions.

---

[57]Conceicao do Carangola Gospel Hall, opened in 1914, is thought to have been the first in the interior of Brazil.

[58]The recently married Mr and Mrs St John left England for Argentina in October 1914.

Mr McNair continued to make long journeys usually on horseback in Minas Gerais until 1933 when he moved to Teresopolis near Rio de Janeiro where he founded the Evangelical Publishing House. In 1913 his *Round South America on the King's Business,* written in English, had been published in London. Now he became busy with his pen in Portuguese. His works include *The Bible Explained, Small Bible Dictionary* and *Occasional Letters*.

A major legacy for Brazilian Christians has been his contribution to their hymnology. He translated many English language hymns into Portuguese, and composed others. No less than 157 of these hymns are in a book still in use. A brother presently serving the Lord in Brazil has written, "His hymns are first class, scripturally accurate, with excellent metre and rhyme, and his command of the Portuguese language is amazing. You would never think he was a foreigner."

The long life and service of Mr McNair ended when he departed to be with Christ on 11th January 1959.

Vanguard in Venezuela

Venezuela lies to the north of the equator and its coastline is on the Caribbean Sea. Simon Bolivar, famous in South America as a liberator and patriot, was born in Caracas its capital in 1783. The country, with Colombia, Ecuador and Panama, was part of the Spanish viceroyalty of Gran Colombia. Independence from Spain was secured in 1821 and initially the four countries formed one republic. This did not continue long and in 1829 Venezuela became a separate country.

Here too the British and Foreign Bible Society began the first known evangelical work. A colporteur was in the country in 1854 but little progress was made at first. Around 1880 a Mr and Mrs Bryant came from Spain and commenced a work in Caracas. An assembly of twelve believers was meeting there when John Mitchell came from the West Indies in February 1895. He found a country "wholly given to idolatry" in which the baneful results of 400 years of undisturbed Roman Catholicism was painfully evident. For some months he could do little more than distribute tracts and converse with English speaking people, but then he made a pioneering journey inland to the Cordillera de Merida ultimately reaching the highest town in Venezuela, 7,743 ft. above sea level, distributing tracts and preaching the Gospel along the way.

In 1897 he was joined by Enrique Inurrigarro and they began a work in Valencia, where in the face of much opposition, a few were converted and an assembly was established. It was an unhealthy place, being situated on low and marshy ground. Mr and Mr Ernest Thomas helped in Valencia but had to return to England in 1900 because of ill health. A young man named Edward Wigmore came to Caracas in 1906. He contracted typhoid and died in 1907 only 24 years old. Mr Mitchell continued until 1908 while others laboured for shorter periods. Evangelism seemed beset by difficulties and appeared to be faltering, but another wave of missionaries was soon to arrive, harbingers of *The Dawn of a New Day in Venezuela*.[59]

William Williams (1882 – 1961)

William Williams was brought up in a Deeside village in Aberdeenshire. His parents were devout members of the Church of Scotland or the 'Auld Kirk' as it was known. Their children attended the long 'Sabbath' services and Sunday School to be instructed in their religious duties. William's first concerns about his soul arose at the age of twelve when his grandfather died.

Three years later he started his marine engineering apprenticeship at the Alexander Hall & Sons shipyard[60] in Aberdeen. It was a tough environment and, though he continued to attend church services, he soon fell into the ways of others at work. However God spoke to him through the conversion of an older apprentice. This young man bore taunts and persecutions with such grace

---

[59]The title of a book written by William Williams.

[60]Where *John Williams* had been built, see Ch 14.

that William was convicted and one Saturday evening, after listening to Gospel preaching at an open air meeting, he returned to his lodging and trusted Christ. In 1905 he emigrated from Scotland to Canada where he married, but two years passed before he and his wife were baptised and received into the fellowship of an assembly in Toronto[61].

In Aberdeen Williams had witnessed for Christ, privately and publicly. This continued in Toronto and a conviction grew that he should give all his time to the Lord's work. He was led to see that Venezuela should be his field of service, and on 25th April 1910 Mr and Mrs Williams saw the mountains of their adopted country from the deck of their ship as it steamed into the bay of Puerto Cabello. Their first home was in Valencia. Mr and Mrs Stephen Adams left Scotland that same year and settled in Caracas.

An early purchase was a horse to enable visits to districts and villages around Valencia. The distance to Puerto Cabello was 42 miles, and Williams gained good experience on horseback from his local trips. Tracts and Gospels were well received in 'the Port' giving hope for a future work there.

The coming of George Johnston from Toronto to Valencia in November 1912 was a great boost to Williams. The following January they set off on their first lengthy journey covering 330 miles. It was typical of many others. The men walked, leading three horses laden with Bibles, Testaments, other literature and tracts. The roads and tracks were rough and rivers had to be forded. Accommodation at wayside stops was basic - a simple meal, and slinging a hammock. This was rural Venezuela, where mostly poor folk lived in primitive conditions, in contrast to the larger towns and cities where comfort and even affluence could be found. Often they were well received despite the best efforts of R C priests to turn people against them. They distributed tracts, and sold Bibles, Testaments and books such as *Pilgrim's*

---

[61]The interesting record of these events is given by Williams in *Rabbi Where Dwellest Thou?*

Progress. At one place a storekeeper was advised by his partner in the crowded store not to buy a Bible. He answered, "I do not want your advice on this matter. The priest will not stand in my place before God, as the missionary has said, so that it behoves me to see what provision there is for me in the book", and before everyone he bought it. Towns visited included San Carlos and San Felipe where there are now thriving Christian assemblies.

In 1914 Williams set out from Caracas with Stephen Adams. Between 20th July and 8th October they covered 1,500 miles. The outward leg was southwards, then eastwards to the Orinoco River, before returning by another route. Fresh supplies of Bibles and literature were sent from Caracas to be picked up at different points on the way. At one place they met people who had heard Don Enrique Inurrigarro and John Mitchell preaching years before. The journey was not without its discomforts including malarial fevers, and much was accomplished in very needy places.

In November 1914 a weekly meeting had been started in Puerto Cabello. Interest grew and a few were saved. With this encouragement it was decided that the Johnstons would hold the fort in Valencia while the Williams moved to 'the Port'. They did so in August 1915 and in January 1916 an assembly was formed when 16 shared in the Lord's Supper for the first time. God blessed this work so that by 1938 around 300 remembered the Lord at the time of an annual conference.

Missionary work greatly expanded during those years as other missionaries were called by God to Venezuela. William Williams continued for over 50 years until the Lord called him home in 1961. His life and labours proved his own dictum that "It can be done"[62], by which he meant that the Great Commission, given nearly two thousand years ago by Christ on a mountainside in Galilee, can still be fulfilled.

JB

---

[62]The title of William William's book describing 27 years of serving the Lord in Venezuela.

CHAPTER 18

Ecuador: Operation Auca, 1956

Many can still remember the story of the five young men who were brutally killed by some Auca Indians in Ecuador while trying to reach them with the Gospel. With the pioneering spirit of earlier days and using the tools and technology of their own day, they had set their hearts on reaching that primitive and hostile tribe living deep in the forests. Elisabeth Elliot's book, *Through Gates of Splendour*,[63] tells the story graphically and poignantly. It is worth reading, again perhaps, to be moved and challenged by the godliness and dedication of these men and their wives who undertook this task in the middle of the 20th century when many might have thought that such hazardous trailblazing belonged to a previous age. Clearly it did not, and even in this next century, there are still some somewhere, who "have not heard" (Rom 10.14-15).

But who were they, these five men around the age of 30 who were viciously speared by Auca tribesmen on the banks of the River Curaray on 8th January 1956?

Jim Elliot, born in October 1927, belonged to Portland, Oregon, one of four children brought up to know the Bible and to believe its truth. He received Christ as his Saviour in his early years, and at High School his Christian testimony was clear and bright. He developed skills in architectural drawing, then went to

---

[63]Hodder & Stoughton, London, 1957. Information and quotes from this book are gratefully acknowledged. Elisabeth (Betty) Elliot, Jim Elliot's widow, dedicated the book to the parents of the five who were killed. She died in 2015.

Wheaton College where his direction altered towards languages to coincide with his growing conviction that God wanted him to take the Gospel to a Latin-American country. As a 20 year old he wrote to his parents about his life's ambition, concluding with "all is vanity below the sun and a 'striving after wind'. Life is not here, but hid above with Christ in God, and therein I rejoice and sing as I think on such exaltation". That next summer after a mission to a group of Indians near his home he wrote in his diary: "He 'makes his ministers a flame of fire'. Am I ignitable? God deliver me from the dread asbestos of 'other things'. But flame is transient, short-lived." At the end of 1950 after meeting a former missionary from Ecuador his direction became clear. He wrote, "I dare not stay home while Quichuas perish."

Jim's wife was **Betty Howard** whom he had first met in 1947. She went to Ecuador after Jim had settled there, they were married in Quito, and in November 1953 they set up a base among the Quichua Indians at Shandia, bringing in all their belongings in four canoes. Their daughter Valerie was 10 months old when her father was killed.

Pete Fleming was born in Seattle, Washington in November 1928[64]. He was the youngest of the five. Saved at the age of 13 his life too became focussed on Christ and living for Him. He studied philosophy at the University of Washington and although his faith was sometimes challenged, he came back to rest on the eternal truth of God's Word. He had corresponded with Jim Elliot and they had shared some time in Bible study conferences, so it was no surprise when Pete too felt the call of God to Ecuador. He wrote to **Olive Ainslie**, his fiancée, "A call is nothing more nor less than obedience to the will of God, as God presses it home to the soul by whatever means He chooses." He would go to Ecuador without her at first, returning to marry her in June

---

[64]His grandfather, Inglis Fleming emigrated from England in 1926 to serve the Lord full-time in USA, called home in 1955. He is the author of Hymn 587 in *The New Believers Hymn Book* (2018).

1954. She would be only three months in the jungle with him before he was killed.

Pete and Jim sailed together in February 1952 from San Pedro, California, on the *Santa Juana* for an 18 day voyage to Guayaquil, Ecuador, then by plane to Quito at 9,300 ft, there to brush up their Spanish, before travelling by bus up to the Quichuas' villages and Shandia, the mission station where Dr Wilf Tidmarsh had been working for some time. Later they established a base at Puyupungu and in 1954 were reporting that a few Indians had been saved and baptised.

Nate Saint, the oldest of the five, was born in August 1923. He was a Missionary Aviation Fellowship (MAF) pilot stationed at Shell Mera, an abandoned oil exploration base at the edge of the mountains when Jim and Pete arrived. He came from Philadelphia, brought up in a devout Christian family and converted early in life. He was always keen on planes and flying, but at the age of 13 all this seemed to be blocked when he contracted osteomyelitis in his leg. High School became too constrictive for him and he took a job in a welding shop, then learned to fly small planes at a local airport. He next signed up as an Air Force cadet, but just on the eve of his first military flying course his leg injury flared up – his ambitions crashed yet again! After recovery in hospital he became part of an Air Force maintenance crew. A year later he clearly heard God's call to mission work. On an Air Force job in California he met the two ex-navy pilots who had founded the MAF and his future course was set. He wrote, "The old life of chasing things that are of a temporal sort seemed absolutely insane."

He married **Marj Farris**, a nurse he met in California, and in September 1948 he flew a MAF plane to Equador along with another pilot. Marj followed later and they set up home at Shell Mera. There he adapted planes and developed routes over the jungle to serve missionaries and deal with medical emergencies while she maintained essential radio contact for all the flying schedules. They had a little girl called Kathy and a boy called Steve who was five years old in 1956.

Ed McCully, born in Milwaukee in January 1927, was the eldest son of a bakery executive who was a preacher of the Word of God. Ed went to Wheaton College to study economics and became popular as a fast athlete, an eloquent speaker, and class president. From Wheaton he entered the Law School at Marquette University, but in September 1950 at the start of his second year he wrote to his classmate Jim Elliot, "I've one desire now – to live a life of reckless abandon for the Lord, putting all my energy and strength into it. Maybe He'll send me to some place where the name of Jesus Christ is unknown." And he finished with, "and brother, I'm really praying for you too as you're making preparation to leave. I only wish I were going with you."

He met and married **Marilou Holboth** at Pontiac, Michigan, then did a year at the School of Missionary Medicine in Los Angeles before they sailed for Ecuador in December 1952 with their eight months old son Stevie. They lived in Quito for a time, learning Spanish, then moved to Shandia to join the others, later moving out to Arajuno on the edge of Auca territory.

Roger Youderian was born in January 1924, the seventh child in a Christian ranching family in Montana. When aged nine he contracted polio which partly crippled him, but he persevered through High School into Montana State College, planning to become a teacher in agriculture. In 1943 he enlisted in the Army and became a paratrooper stationed in England where he became an assistant to the Army Chaplain. He survived the Rhine jump in 1944 and was decorated for action at the Battle of the Bulge. Not long after this he wrote to his mother, "Ever since I accepted Christ as my personal Saviour last fall and wanted to follow Him ... I've felt the call to missionary work after my release from Service."

Back in Montana he met **Barbara Orton** who was studying Christian education with a view to the mission field. They enrolled on a missionary medicine course together, were engaged at Easter 1951 and got married in September. In January 1953 they went to Equador with six months old Beth, first to study

Spanish in Shell Mera. Then it was to Macuma to work alongside Frank and Marie Drown among the Jivaros (in)famous for their head-shrinking habit. It was a dangerous place, but for more than a year they lived among these strange people, visiting them, trying to learn their language, trying to teach them to read, urgently seeking their present and eternal welfare. But Roger and Barbara were keen to move on to a place where the Gospel was as yet unheard, knowing that the Drowns could continue the work there. Strange to say, also at this time, Roger was having serious misgivings about his missionary work and lack of outward results. He contemplated going back to USA but God intervened and he agreed to link up with the others.

The Aucas

This tribe said to be 'born killers' was feared by every neighbouring Quichua. They fiercely resisted any approach, were untamed by any government and mostly ignored by the outside world. They fought using sharp hard wood spears, trained from boyhood to aim with deadly accuracy. Their 'uniform' was no clothing whatever except large plugs of balsa wood in their earlobes. Perhaps their total hostility to others, especially white men, resulted from the cruelty and ruthlessness of rubber prospectors who raided and plundered their jungle homes during the 19th century. The Shell Oil Company prospected there during the 1940s and in spite of real efforts to be friendly, several of their employees were killed by Aucas. From Shell Mera, Nate Saint often flew his plane over their territory and spotted a few settlements, stirring him with a desire to reach them, an aspiration now strongly shared by the others in the middle of 1955.

They tried to learn all they could about this unusual people, particularly their language without which any contact would be futile. Dayuma, a young Auca woman who had escaped a family killing in the tribe some years before had been accepted into a Quichua family, and with her help they gradually built up a basic set of phrases with which they hoped to communicate and build confidence.

Towards the end of 1955 plans had crystallised and the five missionary families were united in their desire to 'attempt the impossible', believing that "with God all things are possible": the McCullys at Arajuno nearest the Aucas, the Elliots at Shandia, the Flemings at Puyupungu, the Youderians at Macuma farther away, and the Saints at Shell Mera, the hub of operations from which the vital flights would be made in a little yellow MAF Piper plane over densely forested Auca territory.

The Approach

To get to the Aucas, trekking through the forest and using canoes on the Curaray River was out of the question. It was fraught with dangers from deadly snakes and these hostile killers. So the approach had to be from the air, first to discover exactly where they were. Nate Saint's great skill took the plane safely over and down into the restricting forest terrain. He devised line-drop methods to deliver suitable gifts to those below, then sign language and Auca phrases by loudspeaker when they got close enough. They seemed to be accepted and welcomed, and a few 'gifts' were sent back up to the plane. After several weeks it all looked very promising. But while the distance from the plane to the ground was sometimes less than 100 feet, and the distance overland from Arajuno was perhaps 25 miles, the psychological and moral distance between the two groups was immense. Could it be bridged?

It was time to plan a landing. A sandbar on the river bank looked promising and eventually became serviceable when some big trees in the way were chopped down by the Aucas themselves after gifts were deliberately dropped onto them. It was called Palm Beach, a bridgehead to bring the Gospel to these people who lived nearby. On 10th December, Nate made a simulated landing there and decided it was useable although not perfect. Plans for going in now took on a fresh impetus – actual contact within a month?

The planning included the possibility of failure, not only to make contact but also real danger to their own lives. They would carry a small hidden weapon but would only use it if it came to the worst. To these men, the question of personal safety was not important. The young wives also talked among themselves about what it would mean to become widows. Betty Elliot wrote, "Each of us knew when we married our husbands that there would never be any question of who came first – God and His work. It was the condition of true discipleship; it became devastatingly meaningful now."

They decided that the real operation at Palm Beach would start on Tuesday 3rd January. Nate flew in the four others along with materials to make a "tree house", for safety 30 ft up an ironwood tree, with basic food supplies and a radio transmitter. The heat and insects made for uncomfortable living, but they developed the airstrip and cleared more of the area, all the while alert for the arrival of the natives whom Nate repeatedly invited to come to Palm Beach. At last on Friday three of them appeared out of the forest, a man they called 'George' and two women, all of whom appeared friendly and responded to the welcome. 'George' was delighted to be given a trip or two in the yellow plane, shouting to his friends in their settlements below. At the end of the day Nate and Pete flew back to Arajuno and two of the Aucas went back into the forest. The three men climbed up to their tree house while the older woman stayed for a short while in the shelter below.

Saturday passed uneventfully. No one appeared, and on Nate's flights over their houses there seemed to be fewer people around. Were they on their way to Palm Beach? On Sunday morning he and Pete flew back to join the others and spotted a group of about ten men going in that direction. The excitement grew – they were sure this would be the day when real contact would be made. At 12.30pm Nate called Marj at Shell Mera with the good news, and concluded, "Will contact you next at four-thirty."

The Climax

There was no radio contact at 4.30pm. They waited anxiously

for a delayed message throughout the rest of that day, but by nightfall it was clear that something was wrong. Next morning another MAF pilot flew over the area and at 9.30am radioed that he had seen the plane on the beach with all its fabric stripped off. Two days later he spotted a body floating downstream from Palm Beach. Sometime on that Sunday afternoon, the Aucas had ambushed the five and killed them with their long spears. No one knows exactly how it all happened.

Search parties from the Ecuador military along with local Quechua Indians moved in overland to look for survivors, and the US Air Rescue Service came in by helicopter. The wives waited, hoped and prayed. Eventually four bodies were found and reverently buried on Palm Beach during a tropical thunderstorm[65]. The courage and steadfast faith of the five widows amazed everyone. A week later they were flown over their husbands' graves and grieved silently together. Betty Elliot wrote, "Once more, ancient words from the Book of Books came to mind: 'All this has come upon us, yet have we not forgotten Thee ... though Thou hast sore broken us in the place of dragons, and covered us with the shadow of death'." (Ps 44.17-19)

What next?

Waste? Revenge? Anger? Such thoughts never crossed their minds. MAF pilots continued trying to re-engage with the Aucas. Within two years almost all the widows returned to work among the Quichuas - Barbara among the Jivaros, Betty to Shandia, Marj and Marilou at Quito. Rachel Saint, Nate's sister came to develop the study of the Auca language. Local Quichua believers reached out to more of their own tribes and eventually to the Aucas. The trail blazed by five brave men led on to the salvation and eternal blessing of thousands of these once savage tribespeople. It is poignant to note that nine years later on Palm Beach, Nate and Marj's children, Steve and Kathy, were baptised

---

[65]Ed McCully's body was never found.

in the Curaray, along with two young Auca believers, by Kimo and Dyuwi, two of the Aucas who were complicit in the killing of their father. You need to read what has been written since the events of 1956 to get the whole story.[66]

As for those five missionaries whose lives were cut so short, what was their mission and their hope? Before they set out on their final trip, after prayer together they sang one of their favourite hymns: *We rest on Thee ...* to the tune *Finlandia*. Their last verse still hangs on the air, poignant and clear:

> *We rest on Thee, our Shield and our Defender!*
> *Thine is the battle; Thine shall be the praise*
> *When passing through the gates of pearly splendour,*
> *Victors, we rest with Thee through endless days."*

While a college student years before, Jim Elliot had written these words now well known:

> *"He is no fool who gives what he cannot keep to gain what he cannot lose."*

BC

---

[66]*The Savage, My Kinsman* by Elisabeth Elliot, 1961, updated 1989, Regal Books, USA.

Aucas Downriver by Ethel Wallis, Hodder & Stoughton, London, 1973.

End of the Spear by Steve Saint, Saltriver, USA, 2005.

Part 2
TRIUMPHS OF THE GOSPEL

"Now thanks be unto God,
which always causeth us to triumph in Christ,
and maketh manifest the savour of His knowledge
in every place."
(2 Cor 2.14)

CHAPTER 19

The Great Awakening in North America

In Part 1 of this book we have tried to follow the trails blazed by some of the noble men and women who left home to bring the Gospel to distant lands. We now move from the South American countries of our last three chapters into North America, but still in the western hemisphere, as we begin to consider some great revivals which we see as *Triumphs of the Gospel,* as in 2 Corinthians 2.14.

Conquest and colonisation by Spain and Portugal in South America began circa 1500. It was around a hundred years later before the first permanent English colony was settled in Virginia in 1607. In that interval the Reformation had brought about immense changes in England, the effects of which explain why Anglo America became utterly different from Hispanic America.

The earliest New England colony was established in 1620 at New Plymouth by the Pilgrim Fathers who voyaged to North America on board *Mayflower*. The colonists were devout separatists from the Church of England who faced the risks and dangers of settling in America to allow them to enjoy liberty in Christian worship, free from the forms and traditions of the Church. Their aspirations were expressed in the singing of Psalm 100 when, after a difficult voyage, land was sighted. Joy must have been mingled with relief!

The Massachusetts Bay colony was founded in 1630 when Puritans (with Calvinist views similar to those of the Pilgrim

Fathers) under the leadership of John Winthrop crossed from England on board the *Arbella*. During the voyage Winthrop addressed his friends: "We are a company professing ourselves fellow members of Christ and we ought to account ourselves knit together by this bond of love, and live in the exercise of it." The new community was to be "A model of Christian charity, as a city set upon a hill". Thousands had followed the first pioneers to build strong colonies sharing the Puritan ethos, but nearly 100 years and three generations later the early zeal had waned, though Puritan ideals remained tenacious.

Jonathan Edwards (1703 – 1758)

Into such a society Jonathan Edwards was born in East Windsor, Connecticut in October 1703. His father Timothy Edwards, a Harvard graduate, was the village pastor. His mother Esther was the daughter of the redoubtable minister Solomon Stoddard. Jonathan was schooled at home and his exceptional ability soon became apparent. When aged thirteen he was sent to the recently established Yale College in New Haven where he studied theology and philosophy in preparation for the ministry. As a child Edwards had experienced religious desires, but as he grew older he felt himself to be spiritually lacking. In his *Personal Narrative* he confessed that his mind had been full of objections against the teaching that God sovereignly chooses some to salvation. After graduation Edwards served for a short time as a tutor at Yale. Facing problems with his students he suffered a period of severe depression, but this led to the turning point in his life when early in 1721 he experienced a personal conversion. He became convinced that God had saved him by grace and came to a "delightful conviction" of divine sovereignty, and a "new sense" of God's glory revealed in Scripture and in nature.

In 1726 Edwards was appointed assistant pastor to his maternal grandfather Solomon Stoddard in Northampton, Massachusetts, where he laboured for 21 years. In that same year he married 17 years old Sarah Pierpont. It was a happy union in which they had eleven children. Sarah was the great grand-daughter of Rev. Thomas Hooker (born in 1586 in Leicestershire) who has been described as "a towering figure in the development of colonial New England". Hooker had initially settled in Massachusetts but following a disagreement with another minister he had moved to Connecticut to become a founder of that colony.

A first revival

After his grandfather's death in 1729, Jonathan became the sole pastor. His first published sermon, preached to the Boston clergy in 1731 was entitled *God Glorified in the Work of Redemption, by the Greatness of Man's Dependence upon Him, in the Whole of it.* He had a burden for young people in Northampton, and frequently preached against the sins to which he observed they were susceptible, but this was balanced by preaching on justification by faith. In the winter of 1734-35 a spiritual revival broke out and many of those young people professed conversion and applied for church membership. Edwards wrote: "the work of conversion was carried on in a most astonishing manner and increased more and more; souls did as it were, by flocks come to Jesus Christ".

The style of Edwards' preaching was recorded by one observer: "He scarcely gestured or even moved, and he made no attempt by the elegance of his style or the beauty of his pictures to gratify the taste and fascinate the imagination. He convinced with overwhelming weight of argument and with such intenseness of feeling." He spoke with an even voice, but with great conviction. He shunned shouting and theatrical antics, aiming to impress the listener with the power of the truth and his desperate need for God. This recalls Paul's words: "And my speech and my preaching was not with enticing words of men's wisdom, but in demonstration of the Spirit and of power" (1 Cor 2.4).

Although revival spread to neighbouring towns this awakening remained primarily local. After some months it seemed to have passed and again Edwards was preaching to congregations seemingly dull of hearing. This continued until 1740 when the

Spirit of God moved in a mighty way in the preaching of George Whitefield during his second visit to British North America.

George Whitefield's preaching

Whitefield arrived in Philadelphia in September 1739 where he preached to large crowds from the balcony of the Court House. One day Benjamin Franklin, then a young printer, joined the crowd, but instead of listening he began to walk away, stopping at intervals to check if he could still hear. His purpose was to calculate the number of people who standing in a semi-circle would be able to hear Whitefield's extraordinary voice. His estimate was over 30,000. Franklin befriended Whitefield and offered to print his sermons. He also lodged him above his shop although he was not converted[1]. Whitefield preached in New York before travelling south through Maryland and Carolina to Georgia. In every place huge numbers flocked to hear him and many were saved.

While Whitefield was in Georgia, Edwards wrote asking him to come to Northampton to preach. That visit was accompanied by a wave of blessing throughout the New England colonies as revival became widespread in 1740-42. He preached on Boston Common to the largest crowd that had yet assembled there. Whitefield proclaimed the same message as Edwards, but his style was very different. He used his powerful voice to full effect, gesticulating all the while. He was a gifted orator who could paint vivid word pictures that captivated his audiences. Edwards spoke from meticulously prepared notes, Whitefield with none. The vital thing was that the Spirit of God used both men and others too, in a great revival for the eternal blessing of multitudes.

Jonathan Edward's preaching

Edwards' ministry was again greatly blessed. In July 1741 in Enfield, he preached what became his best known sermon,

---

[1]Christianity.com excerpts from George Leon Walker's *Some Aspects of the Religious Life of New England.*

Sinners in the Hands of an Angry God based upon the text of Deuteronomy 32.35: "To me belongeth vengeance and recompense; their foot shall slide in due time: for the day of their calamity is at hand, and the things that shall come upon them make haste". He had preached the sermon from his own pulpit to no apparent effect, but at Enfield the scene was extraordinary as described by Stephen Williams, an eyewitness. "Before the sermon was done there was a great moaning and crying went through ye whole house… 'What shall I do to be saved'… 'Oh, I am going to hell'… 'Oh, what shall I do for Christ', and so forth. So the minister was obliged to desist, yet shrieks and cries were piercing and amazing[2]." The Spirit of God was clearly moving in great power!

Other preachers

Gilbert Tennent was born in Co Armagh, Ireland in 1703. When he was aged 15 his parents moved to Pennsylvania. His father William Tennent was a graduate of Edinburgh University and in 1735 he established a school for ministers which some derided as a "Log College" but which provided a sound education. It became a training ground for Presbyterian preachers. Gilbert had been under conviction in his teens but was not converted until he was 20 years old. Three years later he was ordained and began a ministry in New Jersey. He was a zealous evangelist and many were saved through his ministry. The first time Whitefield heard him he recorded in his journal "Never before heard such a searching sermon. He convinced me more and more that we can preach the Gospel of Christ no further than we have experienced the power of it in our own hearts. Being deeply convicted of sin, by God's Holy Spirit at his conversion, he has learned experimentally to dissect the heart of a natural man. Hypocrites must either be soon converted or enraged at his preaching".[3]

---

[2]enrichmentjournal.ag.org *Jonathan Edwards and the Great Awakening* by William P Farley.
[3]www.evangelical-times.org/27317/gilbert-tennent

Samuel Davies was another effective Presbyterian evangelist. He became the first dissenting minister to be granted a licence to preach in Anglican Virginia. He was born in Delaware in 1723 of parents who were earnest Christians and who had emigrated from Wales. They had been childless for a long time, and Samuel later wrote "I am a son of prayer like my namesake Samuel the prophet". At 12 years old he came to a personal knowledge of the Lord and at 15 he made a public confession of faith. He wrote the hymn *Great God of Wonders*[4].

Some outcomes

It has been estimated that during the revival about 10% of the population of New England was converted. Inevitably there was opposition to this divine work. Some ministers objected to the "enthusiasm" of the Awakening and what was regarded as the excessive emotional outbursts of some new converts. Edwards stoutly defended the revival in *The Distinguishing Marks of a Work of the Spirit of God* published in 1741. He explained that emotional displays did not prove that someone was a convert, but neither did these hinder God's working.

Lasting testimony to the spiritual power of the Great Awakening was of course in transformed lives. God had spoken, and among those who heard was David Brainerd, the subject of the next chapter. The colonies had a mission field on their doorstep but little had been done to evangelise native Americans. In his few years Brainerd was "a burning and a shining light" (John 5.35), and the example of his missionary zeal for Indian tribes remained as fruit of the Awakening.

In later years problems arose for Edwards in his Northampton pastorate. He had introduced a new requirement that an applicant to church membership must give a credible profession of genuine faith before being allowed to partake of 'communion'. Although this was reverting to former Puritan practice, it

---

[4]www.evangelical-times.org/23576/samuel-davies

differed from that of his grandfather who had believed that 'communion' was a "converting ordinance". A large majority of the congregation rejected Edwards' convictions and the controversy led to his dismissal. On 1st July 1750 he preached a dignified farewell sermon. Refusing other invitations, including one from Scotland, he moved to Stockbridge, a frontier town in western Massachusetts where for eight years he ministered to a small congregation and became a missionary to the local Indians. In the relative isolation of Stockbridge he produced major theological works including *Freedom of Will* in 1754, *Great Christian Doctrine of Original Sin Defended* in 1757. *A History of the Work of Redemption* based upon a series of his sermons was published posthumously.

In 1758 Edwards left Stockbridge having accepted the post of President of the College of New Jersey, later Princeton University. He had just taken up his duties when a smallpox epidemic broke out. Edwards urged his own family and the townsfolk to be inoculated. Many were, and survived the outbreak, but in Edwards' case complications arose from his inoculation and he died only 55 years of age.

He was the theologian of the Great Awakening in America and his writings proved to be formative in American thought. But perhaps his greatest work was evangelism. That was where his heart lay, and God used him mightily in these great times of revival.

JB

CHAPTER 20

David Brainerd (1718 – 1747)

August 19th 1745 is a significant date in Scottish history. On that day Charles Edward Stewart raised his royal standard on the shore of Loch Shiel on Scotland's west coast to begin his abortive attempt to restore the British throne to his exiled father. Many there that day ended their lives a few months later on the blood stained heather of Culloden Moor. On that same day, far away in Crossweeksung, New Jersey, David Brainerd opened his Bible at Isaiah 55.1, "Ho, every one that thirsteth, come ye to the waters ..." Many there that day found new life in Christ.

Two years later, Jonathan Edwards (see previous chapter) sat in his study poring over a small yellowed manuscript with lettering so tiny that it strained his eyes. His feelings as he read this hand-written document were those of admiration, sadness, and astonishment. It told in graphic detail the amazing experiences of David Brainerd as he lay dying. His brief but amazingly fruitful ministry to the Indians of New York, Pennsylvania, and New Jersey was over. As Edwards laid down the diary, he made a firm decision: this must be published. Due to that decision David Brainerd's name is known and revered by many Christians to this day. His detailed diary,[5] which he reluctantly gave Edwards permission to publish shortly before his death,

---

[5]At the request of the missionary society under which he served, he submitted a public journal for publication. This journal (June 1745 – June 1746), and Edwards' book, are freely available online. Both are essential reading for all who desire to know more about this remarkable life.

was put into print in 1749 entitled *The Life and Diary of David Brainerd.* It has been continuously reprinted ever since.

That the story of Christian missions has been forever altered by David Brainerd's heritage is beyond dispute. John Wesley said: "Let every preacher read carefully over the life of David Brainerd. Let us be followers of him as he was of Christ, in absolute self-devotion, in total deafness to the world, and in fervent love to God and man". William Carey, David Livingstone and Robert Murray McCheyne all testified to the impact that Brainerd's life made on them. Elisabeth Elliot said that her late husband Jim, upon reading Edward's book, "was much encouraged to think of a life of godliness in the light of an early death". Countless 'ordinary' Christians have been challenged and motivated by his sacrificial life. The following lines may help us to understand why.

Brainerd's Early Life

David was born into a wealthy and influential family in Haddam, Connecticut, on April 20th 1718. His father, Hezekiah, died when he was nine, and his mother, Dorothy, just 5 years later. He later wrote, perhaps because of this, "I was from my youth somewhat sober, and inclined rather to melancholy than the contrary extreme." Edwards wrote, "he exceeded all melancholy persons that ever I [knew]".

However David wrote of his salvation on July 12th 1739: "At this time, the way of salvation opened to me ... that I wondered I should ever think of any other ... I wondered that all the world did not see and comply with this way of salvation, entirely by the righteousness of Christ". In September he entered Yale College in New Haven, Connecticut. There he first mentions the tuberculosis that would claim his life eight years later: "I was grown so weak, that I began to spit blood".

At Yale he was caught up in 'The Great Awakening'. The college government did not approve of that movement. They decreed that any student who criticised college tutors or attended "New Light" meetings must make a public apology or else face expulsion. In his youthful zeal David did both. His refusal to comply with these conditions led to his expulsion. He later regretted his actions and his attitude.

The Start of his Ministry

A degree from Yale would have secured him a comfortable and prosperous pastorate. The Lord had other plans. He responded to a call from *The Scottish Society for Propagating Christian Knowledge* and in November 1742 was appointed as a missionary to American Indians. In the spring of 1743 he took the Gospel to these at Kaunaumeek, New York State. By this time his health had greatly deteriorated, pain and weakness were his constant companions. He could have lived a cosseted life as an invalid, yet he gave all away to further the work of God. He writes, "Friday, April 1, 1743. I rode to Kaunaumeek, ... and there lodged on a little heap of straw. I was greatly exercised with inward trials and distresses all day; and in the evening, my heart was sunk, and I seemed to have no God to go to. O that God would help me!"

He saw no visible fruit of his preaching while at Kaunaumeek. In June 1744 he moved to the Forks of the Delaware (Pennsylvania) to work among these Indians. They deeply distrusted him, having suffered much from white men. His diary, June 25th 1744 reads: "To an eye of reason everything respecting the conversion of the heathen is as dark as midnight; yet I cannot but hope in God for the accomplishment of something glorious among them."

What was he to do? He frequently called upon God in fervent prayer. Many days and nights were spent in what he called "secret exercises"- prayer and fasting, often reluctant to go to sleep when he felt that he was being enabled to intercede effectively for others. After much heart searching he refused three separate 'calls' from prosperous congregations for he was "resolved to go on still with the Indian affair, if Divine Providence permitted".

While among the Delaware Indians he twice made a very difficult and dangerous five-day journey to reach the Susquehannas. There he became as ill as to believe he would die. In the mercy of God he found an Indian trader's hut and lay there for a week without medicine or proper food until he was able to ride once more. Returning to the Forks of the Delaware, his Indian interpreter (Moses Tautamy) was converted to Christ - the journal entry recording this extends to nearly 2,000 words! The following extract will show how vital this man's conversion was to the Lord's work among his fellow Indians: "He now addressed the Indians with admirable fervency, and scarce knew when to leave off: and sometimes when I had concluded my discourse, ... he would tarry behind to repeat and inculcate what had been spoken."

Progress among the Indians

He had briefly visited the Indian settlement at Crossweeksung (now Crosswicks, New Jersey). In August 1745 he relocated there, although by now so depressed as to consider resigning his position: "I ... began to entertain serious thoughts of giving up my mission; and almost resolved I would do so [if I had] no better prospect of special success in my work.... I cannot say I entertained these thoughts because I was weary of the labours and fatigues that necessarily attended my present business, or because I had light and freedom in my own mind to turn any other way; but purely through dejection of spirit, pressing discouragement, and an apprehension of its being unjust to spend money consecrated to religious uses, only to civilize the Indians... In this frame of mind I first visited [them] apprehending it was my indispensable duty, ... to make some attempts for their conversion to God, though I cannot say I had any hope of success, my spirits being now so extremely sunk. And I do not know that my hopes respecting [their] conversion were ever reduced to so low an ebb .... And yet this was the very season that God saw fittest to begin this glorious work in! .... Whence I learn, that it is good to follow the path of duty, though in the midst of darkness and discouragement."

A remarkable work of God took place. "What amazing things has God wrought in this space of time for these poor people... How are morose and savage pagans in this short space of time transformed into agreeable, affectionate, and humble Christians; and then drunken pagan howlings turned into devout and fervent prayers and praises to God!"

The work was not unopposed. Liquor selling white men, like the masters of the demon possessed girl in Philippi, saw that "the hope of their gains was gone". They attempted to undermine the message by discrediting the messenger, branding him as a liar and deceiver. Playing on the fiercely independent nature of the Indians they said that he planned to gather his converts together and ship them to England as slaves. Their accusations fell on deaf ears. David saw the hand of God in this.

> "God preserved these poor ignorant Indians from being prejudiced against me, and the truths I taught them"

> "These wicked insinuations, through divine goodness overruling …. only served to engage the affections of the Indians more firmly to me."

Powerful and greatly feared 'Pow-wows' (the Indian equivalent to 'medicine men' and 'witch doctors' in other cultures) vehemently opposed Brainerd's work. Singling out those who had recently confessed Christ, they would publicly dance in a threatening manner around them. Brainerd rejoiced to observe these new converts remaining true to Christ in spite of the Pow-wows' efforts to terrify and humiliate them.

A church was formed of which he wrote, "I know of no assembly of Christians where there seems to be so much of the presence of God, where brotherly love so much prevails, and where I should so much delight in the public worship of God, in general, as in my own congregation; although not more than nine months ago, they were worshipping devils and dumb idols under the power of pagan darkness and superstition."

Final Days

Rapidly deteriorating health forced him to leave his beloved Indians (his brother, John, took his place) and return to Massachusetts. He was nursed in Northampton by 17 year old Jerusha Edwards in the home of her father Jonathan who wrote: "We had opportunity for much acquaintance and conversation with him, and to show him kindness in such circumstances, and to see his dying behaviour, to hear his dying speeches, to receive his dying counsels, and to have the benefit of his dying prayers."

On Thursday, October 8th 1747, John came to visit his brother. Despite David's agonising pain they conversed long into the night concerning the Indian congregation that was so dear to his heart. Around 6am, he murmured his last words "I shall soon be in Glory, I shall soon glorify God with the angels".

David Brainerd was saved when he was 21, and was only 29 when he died[6]. His simple gravestone reads:

A FAITHFUL AND LABORIOUS MISSIONARY TO THE

STOCKBRIDGE, DELAWARE AND SUSQUEHANNA TRIBES OF INDIANS.

Why then has David Brainerd's short life made such an impact on so many? A final quotation from his pen goes a long way towards answering this question:

"Never think that you can live to God in your own power or strength; but always look to Him for assistance, yea, for all strength and grace."

AW[7]

---

[6]"Brainerd's life is a vivid, powerful testimony to the truth that God can and does use weak, sick, discouraged, beat-down, lonely, struggling saints, who cry to Him day and night, to accomplish amazing things for His glory." (John Piper)

[7]Thanks to Allan Wilson for writing this chapter

CHAPTER 21

The Great Awakening in Britain

18ᵗʰ Century Britain

By the standards of modern times, life in the 18ᵗʰ century was hard and often short, nevertheless through the course of that century gradual changes and improvements were brought to the lives of people in Great Britain and Ireland. The Agrarian Revolution, already well underway, increased food production, both from crops and livestock. This sustained a steady increase in population, particularly after 1740. The estimated population of Great Britain in 1700 had been 6.5 million. The first official census of 1801 counted a population of 10.5 million, with that of Ireland being circa 5 million.

The benefits of improving practices in agriculture gave impetus to the emerging Industrial Revolution in the latter part of the century, and to increasing urbanisation. In the view of eminent philosophers and economists of *The Enlightenment* such as the Scots David Hume (1711 – 1776) and Adam Smith (1723 – 1790) mankind was set fair to emerge from the shadows of superstition and religion to a better life guided by science and rational thinking. That view ignored spiritual and eternal realities. Consider this quotation from Adam Smith author of *Wealth of Nations. "*Virtue is more to be feared than vice, because its excesses are not subject to the regulation of conscience*"*. Yet in an irreligious age of increasing atheism and materialism, there was ample empirical evidence to dispute that assertion. Consciences were often seared and silent, and the lives of many, both rich and poor, were scarred and ruined by profligacy and vice.

Moral and Spiritual Needs

A vivid commentary of society in early 18th century Britain can be seen in the engravings of William Hogarth (1697 – 1764). These pictured life in London which had become by far the largest metropolis in Europe with a population of about 700,000. Whilst its very size and teeming life tended to highlight society's ills, similar problems existed in provincial towns and cities. A famous engraving entitled *Gin Lane* depicted a horrific scene, in the foreground of which a drunken woman allowed her baby to fall to its death. This was reputed to be based upon the notorious instance of a woman who strangled her infant so that she could sell its clothes to obtain money to buy gin. Various series of Hogarth's engravings illustrated moral lessons e.g., *A Rake's Progress,* and *Industry and Idleness.* Others were satirical.

The spiritual needs of the populace were hardly met by the established churches. Many clerical positions were merely sinecures, and the wide use of patronage in the appointment of clergy resulted in many incumbents being totally unfitted for their posts. Among other doctrinal errors Deism had been adopted by many intellectuals. Deists taught that men could only know God by creation and observation. They wholly rejected the fact of revelation and the divine inspiration of scripture. Many sermons preached were merely bland philosophy. The eminent jurist Sir William Blackstone visited all of the major churches in London and has been quoted as stating "I did not hear a single discourse which had more Christianity in it than the writings of Cicero".

George Whitefield

Having described the moral and spiritual gloom that pervaded the country, it is a joy to record the immense power and grace of God that transformed the lives of multitudes by revival "in the midst of the years" (Hab 3.2). The revival in North America had its counterpart in the Old Country and George Whitefield was an instrument in God's hand on both sides of the Atlantic. An early feature of revival in Britain was open-air preaching in which Whitefield and Howell Harris in Wales were pioneers. Following his first visit to America Whitefield found that many churches were closed to him and he simply concluded that if he was barred from pulpits he would preach to folk wherever they would gather to listen. Out of doors services, called conventicles, had been a practice of the Scottish Covenanters of the previous century particularly in South West Scotland. These services in which Covenanting ministers preached to their flocks had been in remote or secluded places for fear of the authorities. Whitefield's open air evangelism in towns and in the countryside was altogether new and many of those who listened would never otherwise have heard the Gospel preached. From the beginning he experienced a real power, but this was not without much prayer and study. An early instance was in February 1739 at Kingswood Hill near Bristol where Whitefield, only 25 years of age, preached to around 200 rough and ready miners. Soon he was preaching to huge congregations that could never have been accommodated in a church building. Large numbers were professing salvation and proving their reality in changed lives.

Many in the religious establishment scorned and ridiculed the poor and unlettered folk who heard and believed the Gospel, but as in the days of the Lord's ministry the Father had "hid these things from the wise and prudent, and hast revealed them unto babes" (Matt 11.25; Lk 10.21). A favourite preaching location of Whitefield's was just outside London at Moorfields where supporters of the work later erected a wooden building for services. There was normally no designated time for the service but whenever he began to preach multitudes came to hear.

In July 1741 Whitefield made his first visit to Scotland. In Glasgow many were brought under conviction and at nearby Cambuslang he preached for an hour and a half to his largest ever congregation[8]. Scotland was spiritually awakened as she

---

[8]Revival at Cambuslang is the subject of the next chapter.

had not been since the days of John Knox. Whitefield was so moved that he cried out "May I die preaching." Finally he did!

John Wesley

The Lord graciously moved in the life of John Wesley at a most opportune time. He had returned from his short time in Georgia in February 1738 disappointed and downcast, but on 24th May of that year he was saved in a Moravian meeting house in London while listening to Martin Luther's preface to the Epistle to the Romans. It was a transforming experience. Soon after he preached a sermon on personal salvation through faith, followed by another concerning God's grace "free in all, and free for all". Wesley was at first reluctant to preach in the open air but on 2nd April 1739 he began to follow Whitefield's example. One characteristic of Wesley's preaching was his declaration of the assurance of salvation. He taught that with the forgiveness of sins there should also be experienced the assurance of that truth. Through a long ministry he travelled the length and breadth of the country. He enjoyed robust health and was indefatigable in his labours. The Lord used his preaching as a means of blessing to many souls.

Howell Harris

Howell Harris was born in 1714 in Trevecca, a hamlet near Talgarth in Breconshire, the youngest of four children. His father was a carpenter from Carmarthenshire. The spiritual condition of the established church in Wales at that time was even lower than in England. The local vicar, like many of the clergy, was not all that he should have been, yet he had some sense of the responsibility of his office. On the Sunday before Easter 1735 he announced that there would be a Communion Service the following Sunday. He knew that many of his parishioners believed they were not fit to 'take Communion" and he went on to say, "If you are not fit to take Communion, you are not fit to pray; yea, you are not fit to live and neither are you fit to die".

---

[9]www.revival-library.org *The Early Life of Howell Harris* by Richard Bennett

Howell had come to the service unconcerned but the vicar's remark pierced through his indifference and reached his heart like a sword thrust[9]. This began a time of intense conviction and soul trouble until weeks later he found peace. At that time Harris would not have been able to describe his own experience, but he was soundly saved.

He became an untiring itinerant evangelist travelling all over Wales. He had a compassion for souls, and his earnest preaching and fervour reflected the intensity of his experience of how God had dealt with him. Large numbers were brought under conviction, and many were saved. He would preach many times during the day, counsel and exhort converts at night and then write copious diaries. Often he had little sleep, driving himself to exhaustion.

Some Anglican clergy were extremely antagonistic to him, perhaps because he was not ordained, and he suffered terrible persecutions and hardship. Once he was attacked by a frenzied mob and struck on the head with such violence that he felt as if it were breaking in two. More than once his life was in danger. He met George Whitefield for the first time in Cardiff in 1739 and the two men became close friends. Harris deputised for Whitefield at the Moorfield Tabernacle more than any other preacher[10].

Harris shared the vision of Lady Huntingdon for the establishment of a college for the education and training of young preachers. The Countess had shared her thoughts with Harris and discovered he had prayed about such a provision being made. Their common desire was the provision of capable men for evangelism and ministry. Trevecca College was opened on 24th August 1768 and tradition has it that William William's great hymn, *Guide me, O Thou great Jehovah* written in 1745 was translated into English to be sung on the occasion.[11]

---

[10]*Howell Harris and Revival* by Dr Martyn Lloyd Jones, a chapter in *The Puritan: Their Origins and Successors*, Banner of Truth

[11]*Selina Countess of Huntingdon* by Faith Cook p 253

Other preachers

Whitefield, Wesley and Harris were itinerant evangelists, but the Lord used a considerable number of evangelical clergy whose ministry was in the main within their own parishes. A notable example was William Grimshaw of Howarth[12] where revival broke out in 1742. The Lord blessed his earnest preaching, and before long his congregations had so swelled that hundreds were standing in the churchyard. This was replicated in many parts of the country. The conversion and commitment of Selina, Countess of Huntingdon[13] resulted in the Gospel being preached to many of the aristocracy among whom some were saved. The conversion of William Wilberforce was a notable instance of a Member of Parliament coming to faith in Christ. After his father's death Wilberforce lived for some time with his uncle, also called William, and his wife Hannah, both of whom had been converted through Whitefield's preaching. When aged nine they took him to hear John Newton and he was deeply impressed by what he heard although it was not until he was 26 years old that Wilberforce was saved in 1785.

Not surprisingly in these stirring times there was an outpouring of praise and thanksgiving to God. The joy and vibrancy of personal salvation experiences was expressed in many of the hymns written by Charles Wesley. Such were well suited to congregational singing. Our hymnology was further enriched by the compositions of William Cowper and John Newton.

In Retrospect

From a spiritual standpoint the 18th century was bleak and barren in its beginning. Yet from the 1740s onwards the power of revival impacted upon the life of the nation in that unprecedented wave of blessing called the Great Awakening. The term is appropriate, for the country really was awakened from its spiritual slumber.

---

[12]See Volume 1, this series, Ch 19
[13]Ibid, Ch 18

Some historians have suggested that its lasting influence preserved Britain from revolution as experienced in France at the end of the century. Whether that be so or not, it is certain that there were eternal results, and that a legacy of evangelism, theology and hymnology has remained for the benefit of later generations including ourselves.

JB

CHAPTER 22

An Early Scottish Revival

It was 1742. Parts of Scotland were still feeling the after-effects of the turbulent Covenanter movement of the previous century and the harrowing killing times of 1660-1688. Other parts, mostly in the Highlands, were embroiled in the political aspirations of the Jacobite cause which would end disastrously on Culloden Moor almost four years later.

At such a time the Spirit of God was moving in a mighty way in a relatively unknown place five miles south east of Glasgow. It was Cambuslang with a population of only about 1,000 individuals whose work was coal mining, weaving and agriculture. Soon crowds of over 30,000 would gather there from far and near to listen to the Word of God, and it is estimated that 3,000 people were saved that year. For comparison, the population of Glasgow was then around 18,000.[14]

18th Century Scotland

In the 1550s John Knox had shaken up Scotland and left a lasting impression. In the next century there were revivals at Stewarton and Kirk of Shotts leading to what many called a Second Reformation in 1638 which was part of the background to the Covenanter movement. But in the middle of the 18th century the spiritual condition of Scotland in general was low, as it was elsewhere. Moderatism and Deism had become the norm in the

---

[14]Grateful acknowledgement to *The Cambuslang Revival (1742) and its Worldwide Effects*, John J Murray; www.reformation-today.org

Church of Scotland with little attention to what the Scriptures taught. Sermons were about a lifeless morality instead of the salvation of sinners. Few of the godly Covenanting ministers who had been removed from their pulpits were still alive, and they were now elderly and broken in spirit due to the great hardships they had suffered.

Cambuslang had already heard the preaching of some godly men, among them Robert Fleming, a Covenanter, who was ousted in 1662 and exiled abroad. After him there was a period of stagnation and neglect until William McCulloch was chosen by the parishioners to fill the vacancy, against the wishes of their landowner, the Duke of Hamilton.[15]

McCulloch was born in 1691 at Whithorn in the strong Covenating area of Galloway and found salvation as a lad of thirteen. He attended universities in Edinburgh and Glasgow where he excelled in maths and languages, especially Hebrew. In 1731 he began his ministry in Cambuslang, but it soon became evident that his preaching was not up to the standard of his scholarship - when he began to preach many in his audience left the church for the nearest ale-house! However three "Praying Societies" were active in the parish when he came, and nine more began within the next year.

At this time revivals were being experienced elsewhere, in England under the ministry of George Whitfield and John Wesley and in America under Jonathan Edwards as described in previous chapters. McCulloch was stirred by these great events, and it changed his ministry. He began preaching on the new birth around 1741, the year that Whitefield made the first of his 14 visits to Scotland, preaching to crowds in Edinburgh, Glasgow and a few other towns where he found thousands of deeply interested and receptive individuals, many with open Bibles following what he was teaching.

---

[15]The traditional system of "patronage" gave landowners the sole right to appoint ministers, leading to many abuses. This was behind the "Disruption" of 1843 and the formation of the Free Church in Scotland.

Cambuslang Awakening

Early in 1742 some of Whitefield's converts in Cambuslang raised a petition subscribed by more than half the population requesting Mr McCulloch to instigate weekly lectures. This he began to do on Thursday 4th February. The next Sunday, after he preached on "Except a man be born again ..." a woman called Catherine Jackson and her two sisters left the church weeping and seeking salvation. In the manse many others gathered, more of them weeping and seeking. Catherine cried, "My sins are so many that Christ will not receive me!" "But He will," said Mr McCulloch. "If you are willing to come and accept Him I can assure you in His name, He is willing to accept you." The meeting continued for three hours and many found Christ as Saviour. It concluded with the singing of eight verses of Psalm 103. McCulloch wrote out an account of this memorable meeting and read it the next day to the Prayer Societies who were greatly affected by it and were encouraged to pray even more.

The next Thursday the subject of his lecture was based on Jeremiah 23.6 "The Lord our Righteousness". Many wept and many were deeply stirred. Fifty men and women went for further help and prayer which continued into the night, with at least fifteen finding salvation. News of these happenings began to spread. Crowds came from far and near to listen to the preaching every day. Other ministers came from Edinburgh, Glasgow and Dundee to assist. McCulloch was moved to write to George Whitefield, "Why are you so long in coming to poor Scotland again? For the Lord's sake, do not lay aside thoughts of coming, whatever work you may have in England."

So Whitefield arrived in Cambuslang on Tuesday 6th July. He preached three times that day. He wrote, "Such a commotion surely was never heard of, especially at eleven at night. It far outdid all that I ever saw in America. Mr McCulloch preached after I had ended, till past one in the morning, and then we could scarce persuade them to depart. All night in the fields might be heard the voice of prayer and praise."

The annual 'Communion' was due that month, and Whitefield preached on the Friday to over 20,000 people. On the 'Communion Sabbath' at least 1700 'communicants' partook of the Lord's Supper, and the long summer day allowed at least 20,000 people to listen in the open to God's Word. It was thought that above 500 souls were saved.

Because of this outpoured blessing of God, a second 'Communion' was suggested. Such a thing was unknown in the Church of Scotland, but the Kirk Session agreed - it would be held on 15th August. On this occasion estimates of attendance varied from 30,000 to 50,000. People came from Glasgow, Kilmarnock, Irvine, Stewarton, Edinburgh, and some from parts of England and Ireland. In the open air probably 3,000 partook of the emblems of the death of the Lord Jesus. Worship began at 8.30am and concluded at 10pm as daylight was fading. More than 24 ministers continued to preach to large crowds on the Monday. One of them was John Bonar[16] who had served at Torpichen for 50 years. In his frail old age he took three days on horseback to travel the 18 miles to get there. As he left he used the words of Simeon from Luke 2.29-32: "Let Thy servant depart in peace ... mine eyes have seen Thy salvation ..." McCulloch closed his account of the days of blessing with "May our exalted Redeemer still go on, from conquering to conquer, till the whole earth is filled with His glory".

After-effects

By 1743 the effects of this great revival had spread far beyond its centre. In the early months of the year Calder, Kilsyth, Cumbernauld, Kirkintilloch, Campsie and almost everywhere within 12 miles of Cambuslang had seen blessing. By August, revival came to Perthshire at Muthill near Auchterarder under the ministry of William Halley, and reached Golspie well north of Inverness under John Sutherland when after a year of earnest prayer around 70 people were awakened.

---

[16]John Bonar was grandfather of the well known Andrew and Horatius Bonar of the 19th century.

In the latter half of the 18th century many hitherto cold and formal churches were stirred to evangelical fervour. The Evangelical party of the Church of Scotland emerged under Dr John Erskine who had been at Cambuslang in 1742, and later became well known as minister in Old Greyfriars Church, Edinburgh. For at least a hundred years Evangelicals had a major influence which offset the more dominant Moderatism which was paralysing most churches. "Praying Societies" continued to meet regularly in many places and God answered. These underpinned the later revivals of the 19th and 20th centuries which the later chapters of this book will describe in more detail.

BC

CHAPTER 23

The Ulster Revival of 1859

Matthew Arnold, a son of Thomas Arnold the famous headmaster of Rugby School, has been ranked, after Lord Tennyson and Robert Browning, as third of the eminent poets of the Victorian era. *Dover Beach*, one of his most famous poems, though not published until 1867, is thought to have been written while visiting Dover in 1851. In his fourth verse Arnold uses the imagery of an ebbing tide to lament the retreat of faith in a modern industrial age:

> *The sea of faith*
> *Was once, too, at the full, and round earth's shore*
> *Lay like the folds of a bright girdle furl'd.*
> *But now I only hear*
> *Its melancholy, long, withdrawing roar,*
> *Retreating to the breath*
> *Of the night-wind down the vast edges drear*
> *And naked shingles of the world.*

The poet's bleak and pessimistic meditation seems to take no account of the Gospel of Christ being "the power of God unto salvation" (Rom 1.16), or of God's gracious desire to "open you the windows of heaven, and pour you out a blessing, that there shall not be room enough to receive it" (Mal 3.10). But our eternal and infinite God is not bound by the human condition, or by the current of man's thoughts, opinions, maxims and speculations. Within eight years of the poem being written revival power unexpectedly broke out in America, and then in Ulster with a mighty wave of blessing beyond man's capacity to contain. The reverberations of the 1859 revival would echo in the spiritual consciousness of generations yet unborn, and even to this day.

Firstfruits

Revival in Ulster had quiet and humble beginnings. In the spring of 1856 a lady named Mrs Colville from Gateshead came to Ballymena. She engaged in door to door visitations, with a view to winning souls for Christ. Just a few days before she left Ballymena she called at the home of a Mrs Brown. Two other ladies and a young man were present, and they were discussing the subjects of predestination and man's freewill. Mrs Colville was asked whether she was a Calvinist. Wisely she did not answer the question directly, but stressed the importance of seeking a personal interest in the Saviour and the need of the new birth. The young man was James McQuilkin and for two weeks he had no peace day or night until he found it by trusting the Lord Jesus. Mrs Colville thus became the instrument in the Lord's hand for James McQuilkin's conversion.

McQuilkin was employed in Ballymena but returned to his home village of Kells each weekend. He came under the influence of Rev. John H Moore of Connor who encouraged him and his friends, Jeremiah Meneely, Robert Carlisle and John Wallace, to commence a Sunday School in nearby Tanneybrake. Feeling their need, the four young men began to hold weekly prayer meetings in the village schoolhouse in September 1857. Remarkably that was the month that the Fulton Street prayer meeting commenced in New York. The young men were inspired by three books acquired by McQuilkin, one of which described George Muller's experiences of answered prayer at the Bristol orphanages. After a time two others joined the little group, which had moved to the Old National Schoolhouse in Kells.

On New Year's Day 1858 the first conversion took place and by the end of 1858 about 50 young men were taking part. At the beginning of 1859 the power of prayer began to be known and seen. J H Moore described it thus, "The winter was past, the time of the singing of birds had come. Humble, grateful, loving, joyous converts multiplied…the great concerns of eternity were realised as they had never been before. Many walked about in deep anxiety about the one thing needful; while others rejoiced in the experience of a present peace and a complete salvation".

Fervent Prayers

Two Presbyterian ministers in Ahoghill, Frederick Buick and David Adams had been praying for a spiritual awakening in their community. Mr Buick arranged a testimony meeting in the Ballymontena Schoolhouse on 22nd February 1859 so that converts from Connor could speak about their spiritual experience. The schoolhouse proved to be too small, and the meeting had to be held in Trinity Church. Deep spiritual impressions were made, and people began to pray earnestly that revival would come to the Ahoghill district. Mr Adams conducted a service on the evening of 14th March, but the building capable of seating 1,200 people was vastly overcrowded and had to be vacated. A recent convert named James Bankhead then preached to about 3,000 people from the steps of a house in the square. People listened for hours in pouring rain and many fell down on the street crying unto the Lord for mercy.

Young men including James McQuilkin then held prayer meetings in Ballymena, where by June the Presbyterian Magazine reported "It is not unusual to see thousands assembled for prayer in a graveyard…..or one or other of the spacious Presbyterian Churches of Ballymena filled to overflowing by an intensely serious congregation". Soon the tide of revival swept north to Coleraine. There a schoolteacher noticed a young pupil distressed and clearly under conviction of sin. He advised the boy to go home and call upon the Lord in private. The teacher sent an older pupil who had found peace the previous day, to accompany him. After the two boys had travailed in prayer the younger one found peace through believing and returned to school with a beaming face to tell his teacher, "Oh sir, I am so happy. I have the Lord Jesus in my heart."

In Belfast Mr Thomas Toye invited three young men from Connor and Ahoghill to speak in his church. They had little learning but great earnestness, and God blessed their testimony. In a service in Linenhall Street individuals came under severe conviction of sin. One evening at the end of the service hundreds remained behind and the service had to be reconvened as people yearned for peace with God. On 29th June crowds estimated as over 35,000 persons gathered in the Botanical Gardens for prayer and the preaching of the Gospel. Such occasions must have been memorable for all who experienced them and so many were soundly saved that the character of many communities was transformed. Public Houses were closed and attendances at worldly entertainments greatly diminished!

Characteristics of the Revival

An outstanding feature of the revival was how it demonstrated the power of prayer beginning with the four young men in the little schoolhouse by the roadside and bursting out in large meetings in towns and villages when Christians earnestly entreated God. Their prayers were neither long nor formal, but brief and heart-felt. Another marked feature was that God used humble men and recent converts with scant education to preach to multitudes. "But God hath chosen the foolish things of the world to confound the wise; and God hath chosen the weak things of the world to confound the things which are mighty" (1 Cor 1.27).

As in Whitefield's and Wesley's days hymn singing was notable. Presbyterian congregations had been familiar with Paraphrases and the Psalms. Now great evangelical hymns as *Just as I am without one plea; There is a fountain filled with blood; All hail the power of Jesu's name* were also sung and became widely known and loved. Many dear folk found themselves in Alfred P Gibb's apt phrase, "Out of the mire into the choir".

In the providence of God the summer of 1859 was exceptionally warm and pleasant. This helped the large open air meetings for prayer and preaching that were convened in various parts of Ulster. The preachers were often laymen, and to their credit, many of the clergy acknowledged God's approbation of these earnest men. "The river of God, which is full of water" (Ps 65.9) flowed through the land and thousands were eternally enriched. But among the many conversions, one unusual case caused astonishment, and not a little controversy because of what followed.

A remarkable convert

John G McVicker, minister of the Reformed Presbyterian Church in Cullybackey near to Ballymena, welcomed the revival preachers. He had become deeply discontented with his own spiritual life and was moved by the revival experiences. One night he prayed with his wife, "Lord if we are already Christians make us sure of it; and if we are not, Lord, make us Christians"[17]. Just weeks later on Sunday 26th June, McVicker was saved, seven years after his ordination in Newtownards. It was not that he had been insincere. He had been devoted to God by his parents for the ministry, and when 18 years old he had recognised the importance of the duties of ministry and had drawn up for himself "a form of covenant". Nevertheless he lamented that during years of spiritual struggle "I had never met any person who asked me if I was born again, or who told me that he knew God had saved him".

In light of his conversion he felt it his duty to resign his charge. His profound salvation experience led him to closely examine the doctrines to which he had subscribed. Three months later he was baptised by Jeremiah Meneely in the river Maine. It was a courageous step, for which he was sharply criticised by former colleagues. With others likeminded he formed the first Baptist Church in Ballymena, but as his understanding of Christian ministry became clearer he resigned from the Irish Baptist Society in December 1862. Thereafter he met with believers gathered unto the Lord's name in Ballymena where he preached in a building in High Street and in the surrounding

---

[17] *A History of the Brethren Movement* by F Roy Coad p 171

districts. These developments brought many unjust attacks upon McVicker, and pamphlets were written charging him with a range of heresies. From such false charges he ably defended himself. He later moved to London and fellowshipped in the assembly at Clapton Hall, Stoke Newington until he was called home on 5th January 1900.

Remarkable Preachers

1859 was memorable for the preachers. Ten years later C H Mackintosh wrote to the warm hearted evangelist Andrew Miller, author of *Papers on Church History*, "You and I were privileged to move through these soul stirring scenes in the province of Ulster; and I doubt not the memory of them is fresh with you, as it is with me, this day"[18]. The Holy Spirit's power energised men both unknown and well known. On Dunmull Hill near Bushmills, Brownlow North (1810 – 1875) and two converts from Connor preached to a crowd of about 7,000 persons. When the meeting was supposed to end the people were still so eager that North gave a second message, and throughout the meeting folk were stricken down under conviction of sin. North was the grandson of an Anglican bishop and was related to Lord North, Prime Minister at the time of the American Revolution. His godly mother had prayed for him, but until he was 44 years old he had been a careless profligate. Since being saved in Dallas in Morayshire in the north of Scotland he had become an ardent witness for Christ and a faithful evangelist.

Jeremiah Meneely, who had baptised McVicker, became a gifted evangelist. In the wake of the revival there was great controversy concerning baptism. Meneely saw clearly from the New Testament that only believers should be baptised and that immersion was the scriptural mode of baptism. His example and leadership encouraged others to see these truths for themselves. Meneely became instrumental in the commencement of an

---

[18]*The Life and Times of Charles Henry Mackintosh* by Edwin Cross p 121

assembly of Christians at Ballymacvea near Kells in 1860. After some had gone to Kells and observed the order of brethren already meeting there, an assembly was formed in 1861 in Groggan, two miles from Randalstown, in a little two roomed house warmed by a peat fire. This assembly moved to a more central location at Clonkeen[19]. There was fertile ground for further movement of the Spirit of God and a need to instruct the many new converts. C H Mackintosh editor of *Things New and Old* sought to address such need by writing on relevant subjects in that magazine. No doubt this was helpful to those seeking guidance for their future path, for many hearts were deeply stirred by the wonders God had wrought in their midst.

Meneely laboured much in Ulster and south west Scotland until he was called home on 24th March 1917. One writer commented "he died an old man full of years but with the revival fire still burning in his heart". He was buried close to the little schoolhouse where he had prayed so effectually and fervently when a young man.

A quite remarkable character came to Ulster in that revival year. He was Henry Grattan Guinness (1835 – 1910) the grandson of Arthur Guinness, founder of the famous brewery, who had established the first Sunday Schools in the Dublin area after hearing John Wesley preach in St. Patrick's cathedral. His father John Grattan Guinness was Arthur's youngest son. His mother was Jane Lucretia D'Esterre whose first husband John Norcot D'Esterre[20] had challenged Daniel O'Connell the famous Catholic Irish barrister and campaigner for Catholic Emancipation, to

---

[19]*Brethren The Story of a Great Recovery* by David J Beattie

[20]The D'Esterres were French Huguenots who came to Ireland in the late 17th century. Jonathan Darby of Leap Castle, an ancestor of J N Darby, married Anna Maria D'Esterre in 1693. Her surname appears in the names of some family members in later generations, e.g. Admiral Henry D'Esterre Darby, J N Darby's uncle.

[21]O'Connell was conscience stricken at taking a man's life, and vowed never to fight another duel even if he was branded a coward. He paid a pension to the widow for the maintenance of her daughter for over 30 years.

fight a duel. O'Connell's pistol shot proved fatal to D'Esterre[21]. Henry went off to sea when 17 years old and travelled through Mexico and the West Indies. He was saved when he returned home after a violent storm at sea, and went on to study at New College, St. John's Wood, London. After ordination as a non-denominational evangelist in July 1857, he began his work in London and quickly became a very popular speaker. He often spoke at the Moorfields Tabernacle where George Whitefield had preached, and was offered a pastorate there but declined. During Guinness's time in Belfast an eye witness recorded how he "stood for an hour and a quarter, on a Sunday evening, in a crowd, estimated at 5,000 people, who were listening with breathless attention to a sermon by Henry Grattan Guinness on 'Many waters cannot quench love'".

After his marriage in October 1860 Henry Grattan Guinness and his wife travelled widely for twelve years preaching the Gospel. The couple had a deep interest in foreign missions and applied to join the China Inland Mission founded by James Hudson Taylor. Hudson Taylor advised him to continue at home. He accepted that advice and in 1873 established the East London Institute for Home and Foreign Missions (also called Harley College) for the training of young men and women for missionary work. In 1903 he embarked on a five year missionary tour around the world. His daughter Mary Geraldine married Hudson Taylor's son Frederick. Grattan Guinness was also a prolific author on prophetic subjects and preached and wrote extensively concerning Israel's future. He had a deep interest in Christian missions to the Jews.

But before these experiences of later life Guinness had further work to do when revival came to the city of Dublin as we shall see in the next chapter.

JB

Information for this chapter gleaned from *A Pictorial History of the 1859 Revival and related awakenings in Ulster* is acknowledged.

CHAPTER 24

Revival in the South of Ireland

It should not be thought that there had been no evangelical witness in Ireland beyond the Province of Ulster, for at different places and times faithful men had been a light in the prevailing spiritual darkness. Walter Shirley, Rector at Loughrea in Co. Galway, was converted during the Great Awakening of the 18th century. Walter was a first cousin of the Countess of Huntingdon and became her personal chaplain after George Whitefield's death. He carried on an evangelical ministry in his parish though his bishop disapproved. Robert Daly, Rector of Powerscourt later Bishop of Cashel, was another evangelical[22]. A pulpit erected to his memory in Waterford Cathedral carries the text, "We preach Christ Crucified, the power of God unto salvation". Lady Alicia Lifford, wife of a Dean of Armagh had brought the Church Missionary Society to Ireland, and it was claimed in the CMS Annual sermon of 1829 that the Society had given the Irish Church a "missionary character".[23]

So there was an evangelical Anglican community, mainly within the Anglo-Irish upper class, which welcomed the revival which spread beyond Ulster to the south, when 1859-60 became a time of great Gospel blessing in Dublin especially among the Protestant population. An interesting aspect of the revival in Dublin is that among the converts were some who subsequently made their mark for God, and whose names remain well known.

---

[22]Robert Daly chaired conferences at Powerscourt House in the early 1830s.
[23]*The Evangelical Revival in Ireland – A Study in Christology* by Alan Acheson

Preaching in Dublin

Joseph Denham Smith had exercised a fruitful ministry in the Congregational Church Kingstown (now Dun Laoghaire) since 1849. He was a gifted evangelist, and his heart was freshly stirred by the great wave of blessing in Ulster. In the closing months of 1859 he saw many folk saved in Kingstown. He then commenced meetings in the Metropolitan Hall, Lower Abbey Street, Dublin in which over 1,000 souls were saved in the course of a year. Denham Smith became convinced that he could better serve the Lord free from denominational constraints. He therefore resigned his charge in Kingstown, and encouraged by friends including William Fry and Henry Bewley, continued to preach in Dublin. The need for a permanent centre for Gospel testimony in the city was recognised, and in 1862 Merrion Hall with a seating capacity for 2,500 people was opened. This hall continued to be an assembly meeting place for over 100 years.[24]

It is no surprise that H Grattan Guinness was also preaching in the city for he had been born nearby. George W Frazer, a 20 year old man from Co. Leitrim was persuaded by his brother William to attend meetings held by Grattan Guinness in the Rotunda. Unable to get into the building because of the crush, the brothers climbed up to an outside window to listen. Again on the second evening Frazer could not get in but climbed a gutter and sat on the sill of a second storey window. As his feet hung over the heads of the standing room only crowd, he heard Guinness reading Luke 14.22 "Yet there is room". He went home deeply troubled about sin, and about his immortal soul. This continued for two weeks until he laid hold upon the truth of 1 Tim 1.15. He exclaimed, "I'm a sinner, and Christ Jesus came to save such", and he simply took God at His word. It was the recollection of those amazing crowds that led him to write the hymn *Come! Hear the Gospel sound, 'Yet there is room'*. In later years Mr Frazer published two collections of his hymns *Midnight Praises* and *Day*

---

[24]For more information see *Merrion Hall Centenary* in Brethren Archive.

Dawn Praises, many of which are still sung and enjoyed - fruit remaining from those stirring revival times!

More Dublin converts

George Frederic Trench was another of the young men converted through the preaching of Grattan Guinness. George, a younger brother of John Alfred Trench who became a well-known teacher and writer among brethren, was a student at Trinity College and was preparing for confirmation in the Church of Ireland. He became deeply convicted through hearing Guinness preach on John 3.7, and understood he needed to be born again. He became a frequent contributor to Christian periodicals including *The Witness* and also wrote a number of books.

During his time at Trinity College, George Trench formed a lifelong friendship with a fellow student named Robert Anderson, a son of Matthew Anderson, Crown Solicitor for the city of Dublin, and a prominent elder in the Irish Presbyterian Church. Robert Anderson described himself as "an anglicised Irishman of Scottish extraction". His forebears on both sides of his family had taken part in the heroic defence of Derry in the siege of 1689 by the army of James II. Robert had had a pious upbringing. Even in his early years prayer was no mere formality with him and he had delighted to read Scripture, but at 19 years old in that Revival year in Dublin, he did not have assurance that he was converted.

One of his sisters was saved through the meetings held by J Denham Smith and new spiritual longings were awakened in his soul. One evening he escorted his sister to a meeting she specially wished him to attend, but he left disappointed and vexed. The fact of her conversion still gripped him however, and he cherished the thought that the following Sunday services in the Kirk might bring him blessing. The morning service however left him more discouraged, and he resolved that if the evening one brought no relief he would give up his quest. This is how he described what happened. "The evening preacher was Dr John Hall. His sermon was of a type to which we are now accustomed, for he boldly proclaimed forgiveness of sins and eternal life as

God's gift in grace, unreserved and unconditional, to be received as we sat in the pews. His sermon thrilled me. Yet I deemed his doctrine unscriptural, so I waylaid him as he left the vestry, and on our homeward walk tackled him about his 'heresies'". Dr Hall met the challenge by quoting Scripture and the story continued, "Facing me as we stood on the pavement he repeated with great solemnity his message and appeal: 'I tell you as a minister of Christ and in His name that there is life for you here and now if you will accept Him. Will you accept Christ or will you reject Him?' After a pause I exclaimed, 'In God's name I will accept Christ.' Not another word passed between us, but after another pause he wrung my hand and left me, and I turned homeward with the peace of God filling my heart".[25]

As in apostolic times, converts soon became preachers and Robert Anderson and George Trench laboured together in Mayo, Sligo, Cork and other parts of Ireland with great blessing in the years 1862-65. The character of the work is revealed in a letter from one who, after telling of his own conversion went on to write, "My four sisters and brother, four cousins, and a number of my acquaintances are now rejoicing in the Lord. It does not seem so strange that persons who have made themselves infamous by a life of immorality should awaken to a consciousness of their lost state. But it is passing strange that those who are looked upon by their friends and perhaps by themselves as religious should be brought to thorough conviction that, with all their amiability, morality and religion, they were sinners in the sight of God, being without Christ."[26] Anderson had a distinguished professional career and became Assistant Commissioner (Crime) in the Metropolitan Police. His services were rewarded when he was knighted on his retirement in 1901. Sir Robert Anderson KGB was a prolific author and an able defender of the Truth. He strongly protested against 'Higher Criticism' which attacked the inspiration and inerrancy of Scripture. In *Daniel in the Critic's*

---

[25] *Sir Robert Anderson Secret Service Theologian*, a biography by his son A P Moore-Anderson
[26] Ibid

Den and *The Bible and Modern Criticism* he addressed such matters. Other books of his such as *The Gospel and its Ministry* and *The Coming Prince* are still widely read and have been of lasting benefit to believers - further fruit of those revival days!

The Kerry Revival

Revival spread far from Dublin to the south west of Ireland through the work of three gentlemen known as the "Three Kerry Landlords", William Talbot Crosbie of Ardfert Abbey, Richard J Mahony of Dromore Castle and F C Bland of Derriquin.

Mr Talbot Crosbie was born in 1817 and saved when a young man. The Revival gave him fresh impetus and soon meetings were arranged in his granary that continued for many years with the help of noted visiting evangelists. Mr George Trench married Miss Talbot Crosbie, and settled in Ardfert where he regularly preached. Mr and Mrs Mahony and Mr and Mrs Bland all rejoiced in the truth of eternal life in Christ following a meeting addressed by C H Mackintosh when he preached on the closing verses of Titus 2. Dromore Castle and Derriquin were neighbouring estates and Mahony and Bland had been bosom friends in boyhood. Now they united in preaching to friends and neighbours. In January 1861 Mr Mahony convened a meeting in his Great Hall when he spoke of the love of God and the redeeming work of Christ. This led to widespread revival in the area as blessing spread among the gentry through their efforts. Mr Mahony built a small meeting room on his estate for an assembly composed mainly of his household and tenants. Another assembly was established in nearby Kenmare.

The family of George Needham, a former coastguard officer and a tenant on the Mahony estate was greatly influenced by the revival. George Carter Needham was about 16 years old and may well have heard Mr Mahony speaking. A few years afterwards he went to work in Dublin where he soon began preaching. He emigrated from Dublin to the United States where he became a well-known evangelist and author. He laboured with D L Moody and was Senior Pastor at the Moody Church in Chicago from

1879 – 1885. Three of his brothers also evangelised in the States, all products of the Kerry Revival.

After the Revival

Years of strife in Ireland, the civil war and emigration brought many changes, and regrettably those assemblies in Kerry no longer exist. None the less in those happier times the work in Dublin and other parts of Ireland was both deep and real. A contemporary, the saintly J G Bellett had believed it to be (to quote his own words) "a fresh energy of the Spirit".

The widening circles of the 1859 Revival were bringing blessing and refreshing to many other parts of the British Isles, but as that momentous year drew to its close, the rulers of the darkness of this age were also active. On 24th November, Charles Darwin published his book *On the Origin of Species by Means of Natural Selection*. What a challenge to divine revelation! What a test to Britain!

Lines from Cowper's poem *Conversation* provide a Christian perspective on the writings of these rationalists and atheists.

> *Well – what are ages, and the lapse of time*
> *Match'd against truths as lasting as sublime?*
> *Can length of years on God Himself exact,*
> *Or make that fiction which was once a fact?*
> *No - marble and recording brass decay,*
> *And, like the graver's memory pass away;*
> *The works of man inherit, as is just,*
> *Their author's frailty and return to dust.*

What can we say of Britain 150 years and more since that great revival? Another quote from Cowper (the opening lines of *Truth*) aptly describes its condition.

> *Man on the dubious waves of error toss'd,*
> *His ship half-founder'd and his compass lost.*

Our current challenge is to continue to preach the Gospel. And let us not neglect to pray "that the word of the Lord may have free course, and be glorified" (2 Thess 3.1).

JB

CHAPTER 25

Revival in North East Scotland
(1) In the City and the Countryside

Accounts of past revivals challenge us as we realise how ardently Christians in different places longed for blessing. While young men were praying in the Old National Schoolhouse in Kells (see Ch 23), daily prayer meetings commenced in July 1858 in Aberdeen, the Granite City by the North Sea. It is soul thrilling to learn how God answered prayer in "sovereign grace o'er sin abounding" as the Gospel was preached in various parts of Britain and Ireland "in power, and in the Holy Ghost, and in much assurance" (1 Thess 1.5).

Reginald Radcliffe in Aberdeen

On 27th November 1858 a young evangelist arrived in Aberdeen for the first time. Reginald Radcliffe had been invited by William Martin, Professor of Moral Philosophy at the city's Marischal College. Radcliffe was born in Liverpool in 1825, the sixth son of an eminent lawyer. He had a wonderfully clear voice, which had been used to good effect in open air preaching in the streets of Liverpool. He was a keen distributor of tracts among the large crowds attending events such as fairs, race meetings and public executions (not abolished in Britain until 1868). Professor Martin had hoped to obtain use of a parish church, but was initially disappointed, and meetings began in a small mission hall in Albion Street where Mr Radcliffe spoke to a few children. The Lord blessed and many of them were converted. The change in heart and life was so evident that parents began to attend and were touched by God's Spirit. His gift in addressing children was such that he was invited to speak in the Bon Accord Free Church, with areas reserved for children while adults sat in the gallery. Brownlow North had arrived in the city around the same time for a fortnight's mission, and he sought the active co-operation of Reginald Radcliffe. Their preaching came with freshness and force to the hearts of men and women, and was always followed by personal dealings with definite and growing results. When Mr North had to leave he encouraged all to support Mr Radcliffe's meetings.

Preaching by laymen was a rock of offence to many of the clergy of the Free and Established Churches, but there were exceptions. Rev. James Smith minister at Greyfriars, the collegiate church of Marischal College, was deeply stirred by the work of grace in progress. He opened his doors to the evangelist, and in the closing days of 1858 the work deepened and widened. On 17th January 1859 Mr Radcliffe wrote, "Last night the parish church was filled before we arrived and people were going away. What a sight it was! The building crammed in all directions, and this just to hear a repetition of the simple Gospel. We closed the first service in an hour; recommenced, and closed again within the second hour. Then we retired and took a cup of tea, with something to eat, and returned to the church for a third hour, specially for the anxious. Then we had conversations in the pews – there were too many for the vestry – until twenty minutes to ten. I went home quite fresh; it is wonderful how the Lord gives bodily health. Oh that He may keep me in the dust!"[27]

The work grew until Mr Radcliffe was preaching three or four times daily, and even more on Sundays. Professor Martin, humble, prayerful and full of faith, counselled anxious souls. Early in February Mr Hay Macdowall Grant, Laird of Arndilly near Craigellachie on Speyside, one of the most earnest and indefatigable evangelists of the time, joined the work. Mr Grant

---

[27]*Recollections of Reginald Radcliffe* by his wife, p 46

had been saved when 20 years old, but had been a "closet Christian" for years, enjoying the uneventful life of a country gentleman. All this changed following a conversation with Brownlow North in Elgin in 1855. He forthwith determined to nail his colours to the mast, and began to speak for the Lord Jesus as he had opportunity. He became a striking instance of "a man of the world transformed by grace into a man of the world to come".[28]

Meetings continued in Aberdeen until 18th March 1859. It was a time of extraordinary blessing when many repenting sinners became adoring believers. In retrospect it was recorded that "with tremendous earnestness and force Brownlow North proclaimed in those days the most awful and glorious of all fundamental truths – 'God is'. With singular and persuasive power, Reginald Radcliffe preached – 'God is love'. Mr Hay M Grant with uncommon clearness set forth salvation as a gift".[29]

Into the Countryside

Revival was also experienced in Aberdeenshire and beyond. Dr R McKilliam[30] had just begun his professional life in Old Meldrum, a small town 17 miles north of Aberdeen. He recalled "I was humbled and tendered in conscience, and cast more entirely upon the Lord, when tidings of wonderful revival began to reach and stir the hearts of many. We got together for prayer and a spirit of great expectancy of coming blessing was given to us. Our little town was visited by Mr Brownlow North and Mr Grattan Guinness, before Mr Radcliffe was invited to preach". Of the last named he wrote, "Our brother was with us for only one night. Yet for many months we continued to reap, and the

---

[28]*Mr Hay McDowell Grant, his life labours and teaching*, p 64

[29]Ibid, quoting from *Revivals* by Rev. Mr McPherson

[30]Robert McKilliam practised as a physician in Old Meldrum and in Huntly prior to succeeding to a practice in Blackheath in 1880 where he was in fellowship with an assembly of Christians. He edited the magazine *Morning Star* from its commencement in 1894 until his death in 1915.

place was literally changed. For a long time the ordinary topics of conversation were forgotten in real, serious, spiritual talk".

The final meeting in Aberdeen had been attended by the Duchess of Gordon, widow of the 5th and last Duke, and a sincere believer[31]. She resided at Huntly Lodge where for some months twelve Free Church ministers had been meeting regularly for prayer. She encouraged the evangelists to visit Banffshire where great blessing ensued throughout 1859 in many of the small towns and villages. The wave of revival led to the three-day Huntly gatherings, held successively in the years 1860, 1861 and 1862 in the park adjacent to Huntly Lodge. The Duchess provided five tents, one of which could accommodate 1,000 persons. Mr Gordon Furlong described the scene early on 25th July 1860 when "long and heavily laden trains were rolling towards Huntly, some from the north, but more from the south. The banks of the railway resounded that morning with songs of praise. You could seldom hear the guard's whistle, so loud was the sound of praise. It rejoiced one's heart to see about 4,000 souls gathered to hear God's glad tidings". This must have made a tremendous impact upon a small market town in a rural area.

Duncan Matheson

Mention of Huntly demands reference to Duncan Matheson, another noted evangelist of the period, born there in 1824. His father was employed as the mail runner between Banff and Huntly. His income was slender to support his wife and five children, but diligence and thrift kept them just above want. Duncan received his first spiritual impressions at his mother's knee. Her godly uncle George Cowie, a Secession Church minister, had been thrust out from his church after opening his

---

[31]Her mother-in-law Jane, a striking beauty, was called "The Bonnie Duchess" who famously encouraged recruitment to the Gordon Highlanders when the regiment was raised in 1793 by offering a kiss to every man who took 'the king's shilling'.

pulpit to the famous lay preacher James Haldane[32]. Conviction deepened after the death of his sister Ann, then of his mother. Duncan, who had become a stone cutter and builder, was a strong young man of upright moral character, but restless and troubled. One Lord's Day he heard Murray McCheyne preaching with "eternity stamped upon his brow". Another time he listened to Andrew Bonar preach from Ps 11.6, "Upon the wicked he shall rain snares, fire and brimstone, and an horrible tempest". Solemn thoughts of coming judgment gripped him, until on 10th December 1846 he stood at the end of his father's house, meditating on John 3.16, and was enabled to take God at His word. The burden fell away and he was saved. He wondered why he had stumbled at the simplicity of the way. Further spiritual conflict and discipline fitted him to become a faithful minister of Christ.

Duncan Matheson began his preaching in cottage meetings in Huntly, where he spent much time visiting the sick and distributing tracts. The Duchess of Gordon hearing of his endeavours offered to employ him as a missionary. Matheson had been supporting himself but his resources were exhausted, and he accepted her offer. He purchased an old printing press, taught himself to use it, and soon was printing thousands of tracts. Every moment was devoted to making the Saviour known.

A remarkable phase of his service was in the Crimea during the war there. Matheson did all in his power to relieve the sufferings of the troops in the siege of Sebastopol during the winter of 1854-55. It was said "Never had the British soldier a more true, loving, and devoted friend than Duncan Matheson". His bravery endeared him to all as he distributed Bibles, Testaments and tracts. Russian language Testaments and tracts were given to prisoners of war. Cholera broke out and Matheson contracted the disease. He was close to death but recovered, though his health was seriously affected.

---

[32]See Volume 1 this series, Ch 28.

At the close of 1857 he commenced publication of a monthly magazine *The Herald of Mercy.* Every article, original or selected, bore directly and plainly on the great truths – ruin, regeneration and redemption. God blessed it as a means of salvation to many, and it reached a monthly circulation of 32,000.

In the autumn of 1859 Mr Matheson was preaching in the towns and villages along the coast of Banffshire. His labours were specially blessed in Cullen. Early in 1860 the whole place was moved as with an earthquake. At first the awful shadow of an angry God coming in judgment fell upon many. Awakenings were followed by conversions. On one memorable night he preached in Cullen Free Church on "The barren fig-tree" when a deep solemnity fell upon the people. In another meeting held in a small Independent Chapel, he preached on the text "Remember Lot's wife" and every trifler with the soul and with God was duly warned[33]. Turning inland he visited Dufftown, Tomintoul and Braemar. A contemporary remarked, "There are few parishes in Aberdeenshire and Banffshire where the name of Duncan Matheson is not known and loved, and very few in which he has not preached the Gospel".

He loved to preach at feeing markets[34] and village fairs. It took a good deal of courage to stand up to preach at such events. Crowds thronged the markets, entertainments and stalls abounded, and strong drink usually led to scuffles and fights. Ruffians and ne'er-do-wells would heap scorn and ridicule upon the preachers but Matheson's ready wit, strong voice, commanding presence and lack of any fear earned him respect, and often hostility gave way to a respectful hearing of the Gospel. Many after testified, they were "brocht tae the Lord" at such and such a market[35].

---

[33]*Life and Labours of Duncan Matheson* pp 187 - 191

[34]These markets were held half-yearly in most market towns in the North of Scotland. Farmers agreed a fee and engaged their farm servants usually for 6 months.

[35]Ibid pp 241 - 252

Once he advised another preacher, "Stick by what God has blessed to your own soul. Every evangelist has a something that God has given to him as a great reality, and God uses the evangelist to carry home that truth to do his own work." He was asked, "What is yours?" His reply was, "Ah, mine is plain, Death, Judgment and Eternity; and by God's grace I mean to hold by it." His preaching was "wonderfully attractive but the secret of his power lay in his deep heart-yearning over souls, and dealing with God in secret for them in connection with the sanctified wisdom and tact with which the Master gifted him as a fisher of men"[36]. His business was souls not sermons.

Towards the close of 1861, exhausted by his labours and suffering reproach because of his reproofs of lukewarm religion, Duncan Matheson resolved with a "companion in tribulation" to visit St Andrews to see the place "where the old Scottish heroes fought their good fight". After visiting the site where George Wishart suffered martyrdom, they lay down at Samuel Rutherford's grave and wept and prayed, praising God for all He had done for Scotland and entreating for their country with many supplications and tears[37]. In the energy of this fresh consecration Matheson preached on until his health broke down in January 1867. Though steadily declining in strength he laboured on until he entered into his rest on 16th September 1869. The spirit of the Reformers and the Covenanters had rested upon Duncan Matheson.

JB

---

[36]Ibid p 187
[37]Ibid pp 338 - 339

CHAPTER 26

Revival in North East Scotland (2) On the Coast

Many witnesses of revival in North East Scotland in 1859-60 were struck by the fact that the work was almost entirely in the hands of laymen. Before this it had been rare to see a layman occupying a Scottish pulpit in ordinary dress. Of course the preaching was not entirely limited to church buildings, but many were made available, especially by the Free Church of Scotland and Independents. Some preachers were "gentlemen evangelists". Others like Matheson (previous chapter) and Turner were of humble origin.

James Turner

James Turner was born in Peterhead in 1818, and through him many places on the Aberdeenshire coast were greatly blessed. His parents were poor but honest, though they did not fear God. When ten years old, James was apprenticed to a cooper, at first against his will, though soon he came to enjoy his work. In his youth he lived entirely without God and the thought that he had a soul, that there was a heaven or a hell, never occurred to him. At 15 years of age he was persuaded by his older brother to attend a Bible class. Later he recalled, "For five long years I sat in the back seat, but I was deaf to all that was said, and my heart was as hard as a stone. I often wonder how I did not leave the class, for indeed I did not like it, but somehow or other I could not get away from it".

The Spirit of God was evidently working, and his conscience was awakened until at length he saw himself as a sinner in the sight of God and in danger of perishing eternally. After great conviction and distress of soul he was saved on a Monday morning, 4th May 1840. The anniversary of that date was, ever after, observed by him as a day of thanksgiving to God.

In 1847 he began to attend the Wesleyan Chapel. He wrote, "The Lord blessed my soul, and in the Light of God, I saw it to be my duty to join that people, and among them found that of which my soul was in great want, viz., help heavenward". He became a class leader and earnestly longed and prayed for the salvation of every member of his class. Whenever Mr Turner found a door of usefulness he availed himself of the opportunity of serving the Lord. He was often by the bedside of the sick and the dying, and preached a great deal in the open air. In 1853 he preached above 200 times, attended 260 prayer meetings in which a good number of souls were saved, and all while carrying on business as a cooper and herring curer[38]. In many of the parishes south of Peterhead, Turner reaped a harvest of souls, for example in Collieston which today is a village with a picturesque harbour and mainly holiday cottages. Then it was a fishing community. One Lord's Day he addressed three open air meetings there, at which large numbers attended. He had great liberty in speaking, and many were convicted and anxiously inquired what they must do to be saved.

In 1859 the herring fishing was very poor, and James Turner and his brother were idle for about three months. Turner was thus able visit villages to the north of Peterhead. In St Combs about 300 people attended on the first night. The Spirit was present, and the meeting continued till a late hour. All the next day he went from house to house, and at night preached to about 400. Again

---

[38]Coopers were skilled men who constructed barrels using wooden staves. Herring were gutted by women and packed into the barrels between layers of salt, and the barrels mostly exported.

God came down in power and the meeting was kept going until morning. Many did not sleep that night and neither did Turner. In nearby Inverallochy and Cairnbulg his first two nights bore little fruit, but on the third meeting the Spirit of God came down on many. The same was experienced in Fraserburgh and in villages farther along the coast. He returned home quite worn out in the end of December 1859.

About a month later he set out on missions to Portknockie, Findochty, Portessie, Buckie and Portgordon. In Portknockie he had a very crowded Sunday evening meeting when strong young men were smitten down and became as weak as water. This continued till morning and many were saved. During this period, at one time Turner was preaching in Banff while Duncan Matheson laboured in Macduff.

A slow start in Peterhead

The Lord Jesus said "A prophet is not without honour, save in his own country and in his own house" (Matt 13.57). This was the experience of James Turner for though he saw folk saved in his native town, it was in the smaller fishing villages around the coast that he was mightily used in the 1859-60 revival. Initially Peterhead with its population of around 10,000 seemed impervious to revival. It was a typical seaport of the time, except that in addition to trading vessels, and fishing boats, it was home to Britain's largest whaling and sealing fleet whose hardy seamen and harpooners sometimes made it a pretty rough and tough place! The respectable folk of the town were mainly content with their formal religion.

The indifference in Peterhead sorely troubled Turner and he was not afraid to pray publicly for the unconverted ministers and elders in the Kirks. In the summer of 1860 the Turners' Cooperage – a fairly large place – was arranged to provide seating for about 200 persons. It was intended to have meetings on nights when the fishing boats were not at sea, but soon meetings were being held every night. Sometimes there was little appearance of fruit, but at other times the quickening power of the Spirit was evident. Despite hostility the meetings continued for eighteen months, during which that humble place became the spiritual birth place of many souls. More blessing followed in 1863 when other evangelists visited Peterhead.

James Turner had contracted tuberculosis and suffered times of severe illness. His exertions certainly took their toll particularly in 1859 and 1860. He continued preaching as long as he could in 1861, and encouraged others "to think of the multitudes that were passing into eternity, strangers to God, with all their sins about them, unpardoned and unforgiven"[39]. His last words were "Christ is all!" Thus he fell asleep in Jesus on 2nd February 1863, aged 44 years, only months short of Duncan Matheson's life span. Their lives were short but well spent, when that mighty wave of revival swept through the sea girt and rural communities of North East Scotland.

Turner had been wont to advise converts to read their Bibles. One man remembered "the last words he spoke the hin'-most time he was in Portessie, 'Young men and women I will never see you again in the flesh, and I've nothing greater to leave with ye than this, take to your New Testaments and to your knees'".[40]

Progress in Peterhead

One young man doing that very thing was William McLean, born at Peterhead in 1835 and converted on 1st January 1854. He had begun his lifelong service in the proclamation of the Gospel with James Turner and others. Not a close or alley of his native town, or street of surrounding villages but knew his voice.[41]

He was one of a few Christians who began to meet to read and discuss the Scriptures and began to see that their existing ecclesiastical position was not right. In conversation with a

---

[39]*James Turner or What God* can do p 38
[40]Ibid p 150
[41]*William McLean Veteran Evangelist* by W H McLaughlin. Mr McLean went on to serve the Lord in Ulster and later in New Zealand.

lady visiting Peterhead, McLean said that he was a Baptist. She remarked, "Do you not think that the names given us in the Word of God should be sufficient for a believer?" Further conversations led to deep exercise of heart, as he became convinced of the oneness of all believers in Christ Jesus. The sufficiency of the Word of God, with the Spirit of God as teacher and guide became increasingly impressed on his heart and mind and this led to action.

In 1868 an advertisement in a local newspaper announced that the Church of Christ in Peterhead would meet at No.1 Rose Street. On the day appointed a few believers were seated in the best room of Mr McLean's house above his shop, when two ladies entered. Mr McLean rose to welcome them. The younger whispered, "We saw your advertisement." Her eye ran over the room as if taking in its dimensions, and she continued, "Was it not rather a big claim to make, the Church of Christ in Peterhead, to meet in this room? I believe you really meant, where two or three are gathered together in My Name, there am I in the midst of them." "Yes, yes," Mr McLean replied, "that is exactly what we meant." Thus began the first assembly of Christians gathering to the Lord's name in Aberdeenshire, probably predating by a year or two the earliest such gathering in Aberdeen.

Donald Ross and the North East Coast Mission

The North East Coast Mission was founded in July 1858 by a man from Orkney named Thomas Rosie. One of the early directors was the scholar Alfred Edersheim,[42] then minister of the Free Church in Old Aberdeen. Though directors were appointed from various denominations the Mission had strong links with the Free Church of Scotland. Donald Ross, born in the parish of Alness in Ross-shire in 1824, was its first secretary and superintendent. His godly parents had taught him well but it was

---

[42]Edersheim was a Jewish convert to Christianity. He wrote the well-known book *The Life and Times of Jesus the Messiah*.

the serious illness of a brother that led to his conversion when 15 years old. Before that he had been in his own words, "proud as a peacock, and as empty as a drum". He was a master of the pithy saying! Ross, a firm friend of Duncan Matheson, and like him an exceptionally gifted evangelist, was a shrewd judge of character. He gathered a band of likeminded men to preach along the coast from Ferryden near Montrose in the south, to Thurso in the north.

Donald Munro, a fellow worker, wrote about Ross. "He often visited the places where missionaries were stationed and held special meetings. During these wonderful years of revival from 1859 to 1870, there was a continuous work of grace going on somewhere along the north east coast, often in two or three towns or villages at the same time".[43] For example Footdee, a village at the mouth of the river Dee and within the boundaries of Aberdeen, witnessed revivals in 1861, 1862 and 1869. The clear preaching led to conversions among respectable church members, and the clergy of the Established Church and even some ministers of the more evangelical Free Church became critical of the missionaries. In turn they were becoming deeply exercised about their own position. One Lord's Day Ross was sitting in the Free North Church in Aberdeen. It was sacrament Sunday and he saw on one side a whisky-seller and another on his other side. He thought, "I am surely in strange company and by my very presence with them I am encouraging them to think they are Christians, and thus helping the devil to lead them down to hell. I shall never be found here again."

Growing light and liberty

Early in 1870 he and other missionaries resigned from the North East Coast Mission with its denominational links and commenced the Northern Evangelistic Society. Its field was to be the inland towns and districts of Northern Scotland. Further light broke upon

---

[43]*Donald Ross Pioneer Evangelist* edited by his son, C W R, published by John Ritchie Ltd, Kilmarnock. Later quotations are from the same source.

them when the question arose, what about baptism? Disruption of one of Ross's meetings by young men who were church members caused a lady, who was a true child of God and a Baptist, to remark, "No wonder that they should behave so. Are they not made to believe that they were made Christians when they were christened, and that they are all right?"

It was 'a bow drawn at a venture' and soon afterwards Ross was baptised in the river Dee by John Davidson of New Deer where a few saints were gathered in scriptural simplicity through the labours of Dr Christopher Davis, a coloured brother[44]. It was a momentous step for a staunch Presbyterian whose twelve children had all been christened. Soon Ross learned the truth that the Lord Jesus whom he had long preached as the Saviour of the lost was the centre of gathering of His own. The Mission was dissolved in 1871 so that its evangelists could act as led by the Lord and Ross took his place with a small company of Christians meeting in Aberdeen.

John Ritchie Snr, the founder of the eponymous Christian publisher in Kilmarnock and first editor of *Believer's Magazine*, first saw and heard Donald Ross in Inverurie Town Hall on an April Sunday evening in 1871. He was deeply impressed by "the tremendous force and great solemnity, yet melting tenderness" of the preaching. On a Lord's Day that summer four men including Ritchie walked eight miles to Old Rayne where they were received as young believers from Inverurie. Ritchie remembered, "It was a wonderful gathering, the first of its kind we had ever seen. The place was a country joiner's shop, with whitewashed walls, plank seats supported by cut clogs of wood, a plain deal table covered with a white cloth, on which the bread and wine stood near the centre. There was true worship there that day, such as has to be shared to be understood; it cannot be explained"[45]. Soon many assemblies were established across

---

[44]Meetings in New Deer were held in the house of William Ironside, grandfather of the well-known Bible teacher H A Ironside.

[45]Ibid. This account by John Ritchie appears at p 170.

the North of Scotland as Christians warmed and invigorated by revival blessing, gathered unto the name of the Lord Jesus. It reflected the pattern in Ulster (see Chapter 23).

In this spontaneous and stirring movement, the Spirit of God raised up and fitted men who acted with courage and conviction. They left to us a rich heritage. May God give us grace to enjoy it, and wisdom to preserve it.

JB

CHAPTER 27

Moody and Sankey in America

After the revivals of 1859 and the years immediately following, the Gospel continued its triumph through the latter decades of the 19th century. Thousands were saved in the remarkable campaigns led by Dwight L Moody and Ira D Sankey in Britain and America. These men became household names in their day, and their fame in Christian circles has echoed down the years.

Their early days and conversions

Dwight Lyman Moody was born of New England Puritan stock on 5th February 1837. His parents traced their ancestries to early 1630s settlers. His father, Edwin Moody, died when only 41, leaving his family with scant means of support. With indomitable courage Mrs Moody cared for, and raised her nine children. Dwight began his working life in a neighbouring village when not yet 10 years old. In the spring of 1854 he left home in East Northfield to go to Boston and find work. That was no easy task for a country boy, but two of his uncles were in the boot and shoe business, and he found employment with them on condition that he attended church and Sunday school.

Thus he became a salesman in Holton's shoe shop, and a member of a Bible Class at Mount Vernon Congregational Church, led by a fine Christian named Edward Kimball. Young Moody was self-reliant, headstrong and sometimes over confident, yet Mr Kimball felt a burden for him. One day he determined to speak to the youth about Christ and salvation. He found him in the back shop, and after serious conversation Moody gave himself, and his life, to Christ. It was the beginning of a remarkable Christian life. An engraved stone set in the wall of a building now marks the site of that Boston shoe shop where Moody was converted.

Ira David Sankey was born in 1840 in Edinburg, Pennsylvania. Like D L Moody he was one of a family of nine. His parents David and Mary were pious Methodists and when a boy Ira loved to join the family around the fire in winter evenings singing old and familiar hymns. Spiritual interests were kindled through the interest of a Mr Fraser who took the young lad with his own sons to a Sunday School. He was converted in 1856 when attending meetings at a Church known as King's Chapel.

In 1857 the family moved to New Castle, also in Pennsylvania, where his spirituality and musical talent were quickly recognised in the Jefferson Street Methodist Episcopal Church. He had a fine singing voice which gained that full rich resonant quality which later made him famous. He did not write lyrics like Philip Bliss and Fanny Crosby but was especially gifted in composing tunes many of which are still loved and sung. In March 1861 he enlisted in the Union Army, where he continued his Christian work by organising camp meetings and leading the singing. Two years later he married Fanny Edwards, a Sunday School teacher and a member of his choir. A YMCA branch was opened in New Castle in 1867 and Sankey became its Secretary and later President. It was YMCA work that led to his meeting with Moody and opened the door to the crowning achievements of his life[46].

Moody's life and work in Chicago

After working for two years in Boston, Moody went west to Chicago, the growing prairie city on the shore of Lake Michigan, where he quickly found employment in a shoe store. Desiring to identify himself with God's people, he presented his Mount Vernon membership letter to Plymouth Church in Chicago, and was soon actively engaged in Christian service. He volunteered

---

[46]Information from *Archives, Moody Bible Institute* in this chapter and the next is gratefully acknowledged.

to teach in a struggling Mission Sunday School, and was welcomed by the Superintendent provided he could bring his own class. The next Sunday he brought in 18 youngsters from the nearby sidewalks.

Moody proved to be a real soul winner, pouring his energies into a rapidly growing Sunday School work, and willing to be anything from superintendent to janitor. Remembering the loneliness of his early days in Boston, he sought to contact the large numbers of young men coming to the city for work. This led to a lasting interest in the Young Men's Christian Association. He decided to work on a commission basis to more easily accommodate his Christian work, until in 1860 aged 23 years, he gave up his increasing secular prospects to devote himself to serve the Lord full time. In 1862 he married Emma Revell. It was a union of heart and soul, and in his wife he found his greatest human resource.

The outbreak of the American Civil War brought opportunities for Gospel work among soldiers. This began in Camp Douglas, Chicago, through which large numbers of recruits to the Union Army passed. By Gospel services, prayer meetings, distribution of Bibles, tracts and books, Moody sought to win soldiers for Christ. He travelled to the front lines to minister to the dying and the wounded, and some were blessed and saved on the brink of eternity. Later in the war Confederate Army prisoners were held in Camp Douglas, and many of them were saved.

After the war Moody returned to his Sunday School and YMCA work. His zeal in Gospel preaching became well known in Illinois and in surrounding States. His passion was to win souls for Christ. He did not wait for opportunities to be made, but rather made them himself. On one occasion, he accosted a young man, apparently just arrived in the city, with his frequent inquiry, "Are you a Christian?" "It's none of your business," was the curt reply. "Yes it is," was the reassurance. "Then you must be D L Moody!" said the stranger.

Significant experiences

It was characteristic of Moody to appreciate the gifts and qualities of others, and he grasped every opportunity to invite gifted Bible teachers and evangelists to speak at meetings in Farwell Hall or in the Illinois Street Church. As a result he became acquainted with visitors from other parts of America, and from Britain, and learned of Christian work elsewhere. There grew a strong desire to meet, and hear, men such as C H Spurgeon and George Muller and in 1867 he made his first visit to England. There was mutual benefit for the visitor and his hosts. The latter were refreshed by Moody's direct American ways, and by the lively reports of his work. Once when introduced as "Our American cousin, the Rev. Mr Moody of Chicago", Moody responded, "The chairman has made two mistakes. To begin with, I'm not the Reverend Mr Moody at all. I'm plain Dwight L Moody a Sabbath School worker. And then, I'm not your American cousin. By the grace of God I'm your brother who is interested with you in our Father's work for His children." That must have made folk sit up!

At Bristol he visited Muller at the Ashley Down Orphan Houses, and in Dublin he met Henry Moorehouse known as "The Boy Preacher". The unexpected sequel to that meeting deeply influenced Moody. He thought, "That beardless boy looks little more than seventeen". In fact he was 27 and already a veteran revival preacher. Moorehouse told Moody he would like to accompany him on his return to America, and preach in Chicago, but received no encouragement. Undeterred Moorehouse arrived some months later. Moody was to be away for two nights, and after some debate it was agreed to allow Moorehouse to speak. On his return Moody was astonished to hear that the congregation had been enthralled by Moorehouse preaching on John 3.16. Mrs Moody informed her husband "he tells the worst sinners that God loves them" and "he backs up everything he says with the Bible". Moorehouse went on to preach from that same verse for seven nights. It made an indelible impression on Moody. Moorehouse's preaching taught him "to draw his sword full length, to fling the scabbard away, and enter battle with the naked blade".

Moody and Sankey meet

Another significant meeting occurred during the 1870 Indianapolis YMCA Convention. Moody was to open an early morning Prayer meeting. The singing had become dull and uninspiring until the delegate from New Castle was asked to take the lead. Ira D Sankey began to sing *There is a fountain filled with blood.* After the meeting Sankey was introduced to Moody, who recognised him as the person who had led the singing. Moody had been impressed, and he told Sankey, "You are the man I have been looking for, and I want you to come to Chicago to help me in my work."

Sankey could not immediately do this, but promised to give the request prayerful consideration. He also promised to meet Moody at a certain street corner that same evening for an open air meeting and Moody invited him to sing, *Am I a soldier of the cross?* Moody then preached for about 20 minutes to the large crowd of working men who had gathered, and Sankey thought it was one of the most powerful addresses he had ever heard. Moody then announced the venue at which he was going to speak and invited the crowd to follow him. They sang, *Shall we gather at the river?* as they marched down the street. Later Sankey came to Chicago for a week. On their first day together they visited folk who were sick. Sankey sang a hymn and Moody read words of comfort from the Scriptures. Soon after this Sankey resigned from business, and joined Moody in his work at Illinois Street Church, and with the YMCA. It became a famous partnership!

The Great Fire of Chicago

The spring and summer of 1871 were hot and dry in Chicago. Moody decided upon a series of meetings on the subject of Bible characters, concluding with six evenings on a study of Christ. On his fifth evening he preached to the largest congregation that he had ever addressed in the city, on the text "What shall I do then with Jesus which is called Christ?" He asked his hearers to take this text home and think about it and "next Sunday we will come to Calvary and the cross and we will decide what we will do with Jesus of Nazareth". That night the great fire broke out and Chicago was laid in ashes. "What a mistake," he later recounted, "I have never since dared to give an audience a week to think of their salvation."

Such contacts and experiences moulded Mr Moody, and fitted him to be the vessel used by God to preach the Gospel to thousands in major campaigns in both Britain and America.

Preaching to multitudes

After their first campaign in Britain preparations were made for meetings in American cities. In the years 1875, 1876 and 1877, campaigns were conducted in Brooklyn, Philadelphia, New York, Chicago and Boston. This began 20 years of evangelistic missions in America.

Ministers and laymen invited Moody and Sankey to come to their cities and made suitable arrangements. In Philadelphia a large temporary structure, the Depot Tabernacle, was erected on a disused railroad freight depot with seating for 13,000 people. Very early Morning Prayer Meetings were normal, and each day Moody preached two or three times. On the last evening of 1875 Moody made earnest appeals as the midnight hour approached. He then asked for silent prayer, and while heads were bowed, the stillness was broken by Sankey singing *Almost persuaded*.

In New York the Hippodrome on the site of the present Madison Square Garden was split into two large halls each accommodating 7,000 people. When many were seeking entry Moody would ask Christians to vacate their seats and go to the other hall to pray. The audiences were the largest yet seen in the city. Moody preached in all the major cities in the United States and Canada. Sometimes he devoted an entire winter to evangelise in one place. It was his special work, but he also held

Bible readings for Christians for example in Chicago, always dear to his heart, Baltimore, St Louis and San Francisco[47].

A reflection

One hundred years after the days of George Whitefield and Jonathan Edwards America had been transformed, and in that process the ethos of the early colonists in New England and even of Pennsylvania had been largely overwhelmed. The 13 colonies had fought a Revolutionary War, won independence from Britain and united to forge a new nation. As the 19th century progressed, westward expansion and industrialisation in the eastern seaboard had been fuelled by mass emigration from Britain, Ireland and continental Europe rapidly increasing the population of many American cities. Then the new nation had been wracked by Civil War. Against such a background fresh revival blessing may be viewed as a testimony to divine providence, when by God's grace thousands were saved and Christian testimony in America flourished anew.

JB

---

[47]Information in this chapter, and the next, from *The Life of Dwight L Moody* by his son, William R Moody is gratefully acknowledged.

CHAPTER 28

Moody and Sankey in Britain

The preliminary to D L Moody's first campaign in Britain was his second visit in 1872. He wished to profit from the ministry of respected Bible teachers, and he attended a number of meetings, including the Mildmay Conference. There he met for the only time the Rev. William Pennefather, who suggested that he should make an extended visit. Equally warm invitations, with the promise of funds to meet costs, came from Mr Henry Bewley of Merrion Hall Dublin, and Mr Cuthbert Bainbridge of Newcastle-upon-Tyne[48]. Moody had not intended to preach while in England but the pastor of a north London Church urged him to speak. The Sunday morning service gave little encouragement, but in the evening the atmosphere seemed charged by the Spirit of God. During meetings lasting for ten days several hundred persons professed salvation.

The first campaign 1873-75

Encouraged by this, Moody returned to England the next year. He and Sankey landed at Liverpool on 17th June 1873. Expected funds had not been forthcoming, and after their arrival the reason became apparent, in that all of the three friends who had promised support had recently been called home to be with the Lord. It seemed an inauspicious beginning, and Moody remarked that if a door did not open they would return to America.

---

[48]Cuthbert's father Emerson Bainbridge, a staunch Methodist, was founder of a large Department Store in Newcastle. At a time when shop staff worked 15 hour days, six days each week, he allowed time off to staff, one evening for courting, and two if they regularly attended prayer meetings.

That evening he discovered in a coat pocket an unopened letter he had received before leaving New York. It was from Mr Bennet, Secretary of the YMCA at York, who had heard of Moody's work among young men, and asked him to visit York if he came to England. Moody felt the door was ajar, and perhaps the Lord was leading him to York. Bennett said the town was cold and dead but meetings began. F B Meyer (the renowned devotional writer) then invited Moody to preach in his chapel in York, where they had a fortnight of "most blessed and memorable meetings". Daily prayer meetings were held at noon, and apathy and formality dissipated as Christians were encouraged and several hundred sinners were converted.

Meetings followed in Sunderland where a local pastor noted that Mr Moody is the *Mercurius* of the pair, while Mr Sankey is the *Orpheus*. Newcastle was the next port of call where the mission extended over many weeks. The city became the birth place of *Sacred Songs and Solos*, the first edition of which comprised only 16 pages, including the hymns that Sankey had been singing in Chicago and elsewhere. Within his lifetime the collection of hymns increased, and the hymn book became popular in all English speaking lands.

Henry Moorehouse joined Moody in Newcastle. He observed three notable features of Moody's preaching:

(1)   he rests on the simple story of a crucified and risen Saviour,

(2)   he expects when he preaches that souls will be saved, with the result that God honours his faith,

(3)   he preaches as if there was never to be another meeting.

In November Moody and Sankey arrived in Edinburgh and through the weeks following the city witnessed a remarkable demonstration of the Gospel of Christ being "the power of God unto salvation". The Free Church Assembly Hall and other large buildings were filled to overflowing but the numbers was not the most remarkable feature. It was the presence and power of the Holy Spirit, the solemn awe, the prayerful believing expectant spirit. One minister was struck by the variety among inquirers: "the old man of seventy-five to the youth of eleven, soldiers from the castle and students from the university, the backsliding, the intemperate, the sceptic, the rich and the poor, the educated and the uneducated". He felt it was a sacred pleasure "first to hear the cry of conviction, then the joy of reconciliation and peace". Blessing flowed into 1874, in Glasgow, Dundee, and Aberdeen.

The Ninety and Nine

It was in Scotland that Sankey first sang what became one of his best known hymn tunes. While travelling by train from Glasgow to Edinburgh he read the poem *There were ninety and nine* written by Elizabeth Clephane[49] in the weekly, *Christian Age.* He so enjoyed the poem that he read it aloud, but Moody was so engrossed in reading a letter from Chicago that he didn't hear a word. Sankey cut out the piece and put it in his scrapbook. The next day, Moody preached on "The Good Shepherd", and at the end he asked Sankey to sing a solo suited to the message. Sankey responded by singing the poem he had discovered the day before. Moody and the congregation were greatly moved. It was a fine example of Sankey's musical ability.

Other cities and then to London

In the autumn they visited Ireland when meetings were held in Belfast, Londonderry and Dublin. Moody then returned to England to preach in many large provincial cities. On 31st December 1874 the first meeting in Sheffield began with a new hymn written by Dr Horatius Bonar *Rejoice and be glad, the Redeemer has come.* In Birmingham a witness observed that, "the people were of all sorts, old and young, rich and poor. Tradesmen, manufacturers and merchants, cultivated women and rough boys who knew more about dogs and pigeons than

---

[49]The poem was written at Melrose where the authoress lived and was first published in 1868 in a small magazine *The Children's Hour*. Miss Clephane died in 1869 aged thirty-eight.

they knew about books". The final mission was to London where meetings began on 9th March 1875. Four large venues were secured in different parts of the city and a tremendous work was done as folk from all strata of society heard the Gospel. Mr W E Gladstone attended at least one meeting, and the Lord Chancellor declared, "The simplicity of that man's preaching, and the clear manner in which he sets forth salvation in Christ, is to me the most striking and the most delightful thing I ever knew in my life." It is difficult to imagine such a statement being made by a public figure today. Mr Spurgeon gave his hearty support, and Moody preached in the Metropolitan Tabernacle to the college students on the text "Prepared unto every good work".

Dr Andrew Bonar came to London to help and encourage. His diary records, "At Camberwell Hall not less than 9,000 assembled, morning, noon, and night. In the morning, before eight o'clock, I was summoned away to the overflow in the neighbouring church. But the most remarkable part of the day was our Bible reading with Mr. Moody in the forenoon; about 30 Christian friends present. We were like Acts 20.7, talking for two hours and then dispensing the Lord's Supper. Mr. Moody closed with prayer. Most solemn scene, never to be forgotten".

When he returned to America Moody was asked who had helped him most in London. He replied, "Dr Andrew Bonar and Lord Cairns. The first one helped me by inspiring hints of Bible truth for my sermons; the other one by coming often to hear me, for the people said that if the Lord Chancellor came to my meetings they had better come too."

Later campaigns

The second British campaign commenced in the autumn of 1881 in Newcastle. As before, Moody moved on to Scotland to preach in Edinburgh for six weeks, after which he laboured in Glasgow and its environs for five months. A new feature was the convening of special meetings for children on Saturday mornings. Moody then travelled throughout Scotland, and preached in many of the smaller towns. The winter months of 1882-83 were fully occupied by missions throughout Ireland, Wales and England, concluding in Liverpool in April 1883.

Moody then sailed to America to meet responsibilities there, promising to return for an extended mission in London. This began on 4th November and continued for eight months. In 1875 meetings had been held in a few very large venues, but in 1883-84 temporary halls were erected at 11 different sites, the object being to get nearer to the people, especially the poor in their crowded districts. During these months Moody spoke at least twice each day, and occasionally four or even five times. It was estimated that he spoke to over two million people. It was a time of great blessing.

The third lengthy visit to the British Isles was made in 1891-92 in response to an invitation in the form of a memorial signed by 2,500 people from 50 towns and cities in Scotland. An itinerary was arranged in which meetings were held in 100 Scottish locations including Wick in the far north where on Christmas Day 1891 he held an afternoon Bible reading and a large evening Gospel meeting. It was no holiday!

After meetings in many parts of England and Ireland, there was a concluding eight day mission in the Metropolitan Tabernacle. The students of Spurgeon's College were called upon to assist. One of them, F W Boreham, recounted something very interesting[50]. "Each student was allotted a little block of seats. We were carefully instructed as to the way in which we were to shepherd the people in those pews. We were to see that everyone was comfortable; that everyone was supplied with a hymn-book; and that, without undue button-holing, those who needed individual counsel could readily find it. I like to remember that, among those who attended the afternoon meetings, and who occupied a front seat in the section apportioned to me, was a stately young lady in black who listened to Mr Moody with marked reverence, and the very closest attention. We knew her then as Princess May,

---

[50] F W Boreham, *My Pilgrimage* pp 96-97

the daughter of the Duke and Duchess of Teck, but I have lived to see her become, in turn, the Duchess of York, the Princess of Wales, the Queen of England, and the venerable Queen-Mother[51] – an altogether regal figure, universally honoured and greatly beloved". What a great insight this is into the influence of the Gospel within our Royal family, and an appreciation of the lasting effects of such wonderful times of blessing.

Perils on the sea

In November 1892 Mr Moody and his son embarked at Southampton on the North German Lloyd steamer *Spree.* Three days into the voyage the propeller shaft broke, and the resulting damage to the stern tube caused serious flooding in the after compartments. The vessel was helpless and in danger of foundering in the stormy weather.

In these anxious circumstances the Captain gave Moody permission to speak in the saloon. Clasping a pillar to steady himself he read Psalm 91. Verse 11 touched him deeply as he prayed that God would still the raging of the sea and bring them to a safe haven. Psalm 107.20-31 was also read and a German seaman translated for the benefit of his countrymen. Three days passed before distress rockets were seen by *Huron* a much smaller steamer bound for Liverpool. A tow line was secured and in calmer weather a seven day tow to Queenstown[52] began. It was a dramatic postscript to Moody's last campaign in Britain but a merciful deliverance for all.

Closing years

Though suffering heart problems, Moody continued preaching to the end of his days. He returned home from his final meetings in Kansas City in November 1899, and left for heaven on 22nd December. In that year Sankey made his final visit to Britain,

---

[51]This was Queen Mary, our present Queen's grandmother, who died in March 1953.
[52]Now named Cobh

holding services of "Sacred Song and Story" in 30 towns and cities. From 1903 his health deteriorated until he too was called into the Lord's presence on 13th August 1908. Neither lived long lives, yet how much they achieved!

JB

CHAPTER 29

Revival in London
C H Spurgeon (1834 -1892)

While Moody and Sankey were leading mighty revivals in the USA, and through them many parts of Britain had also seen great blessing (see previous chapters), a work of God was being developed in London which would impact that city and influence many others for years to come. It was being led and expanded by a young man whose name is well known and respected to this day, Charles Haddon Spurgeon[53].

Victorian Britain was prospering, at least outwardly. The great city of London led the way. Expansion of empire, successful trade and commerce, naval and military strength and ambitious building programmes were all making their mark on the major cities with connecting road and rail transport systems developing at an unprecedented rate. But just beneath the surface, poverty, crime and vice continued, with the large cities leading the way in these as well. Religious life in general was deteriorating into formalism. New atheistic ideas seeded by Darwin and promoted by others were spreading fast among the intellectuals. The impacts of the earlier revivals under Wesley and Whitfield were now a fading memory in most places.

Into such a scene came the young, gifted Spurgeon. He had begun his preaching career at the age of 17 in the country village

---

[53]The surname is continental. His 17th century ancestors escaped to England due to persecution for their Protestant faith.

of Waterbeach near Cambridge where he saw the congregation of the Baptist Chapel increase from around 40 to over 400 within a few months. Then at the age of 19 he was invited to London's largest Baptist Church where tremendous blessing would be experienced under his ministry. He would continue there from 1854 until the end of his life.

The Metropolitan Tabernacle

The Church to which he came was in New Park Street, in an industrial and grimy part of the city south of the Thames. It had seating for 1,200, but his first audience numbered less than 200. Soon, however, crowds were squeezing in as the style and impact of his preaching made its mark. The place became overcrowded and so unbearably hot and airless that it had to be enlarged. During the renovations, services were held in Exeter Hall which held 4,000. It was still too small for all who wanted to attend.

Not unexpectedly, Spurgeon and his work attracted many critics from the popular newspapers and from some religious establishments. He was denied the use of Exeter Hall, so then he decided to use the Surrey Gardens Music Hall which held 8,000. However, a tragic accident occurred there when an overcrowded balcony collapsed and several people were killed and others injured. This incident added to the wave of criticism, some of it cruelly warped and unjust.

The new Metropolitan Tabernacle was built at a cost of £31,000 with seating for 5,000 people. At the first service on 31st March 1861 around 6,000 people packed in. Soon he was asking members of the church to stay away from the evening services to allow unsaved ones to attend, and they did. In the next three months around 270 people were baptised and added to the church following clear evidence of salvation and a changed lifestyle which Spurgeon regularly required in applicants for church fellowship. The work of God at his hands went from strength to strength. His preaching was thoroughly Christ centred, Cross based, and backed up by much fervent prayer.

When the Tabernacle needed redecoration six years later, 20,000 attended services in the Agricultural Hall in the north of London. The largest audience he addressed was in the Crystal Palace at a "Service of National Humiliation" over the mutiny in India against Britain's rule: 23,654 were counted in. He deplored the heavy handed retributions in India and called for national repentance, reminding all that "righteousness exalteth a nation". Such a Service, and such numbers and growth in church fellowships can hardly be imagined in the UK today. Do we ever wonder why?

C H Spurgeon's Early Life

Many biographies of Mr Spurgeon have been written[54]. Here are just a few of the highlights of this remarkable life and ministry.

He was born on 19th June 1834 in Kelvedon, Essex, the first of three children of John and Eliza Spurgeon. His upbringing was strongly influenced by his godly parents and grandparents, including access to his grandfather's theological books which early in life he loved to explore, and by his mother's earnest prayers for his salvation. His schooling was mostly in Colchester where he excelled in the usual diet of classics and maths, then for a final year at Maidstone where his strong upright character developed both independence and courage. For all his godly upbringing, Charles was not saved, and he knew it. He earnestly sought salvation and was deeply convicted about his sin. He tried to find out what he had to do. He wanted to feel something. Listening to many different preachers made no difference.

The story of his conversion is well known – he retold it himself so often during later years. One Sunday morning in December 1849 a snowstorm made him turn into a small, almost empty Methodist chapel. The usual preacher was snowed up, so a working man who was there took the pulpit with Isaiah 45.22 as his text. He simply reiterated it with emphasis, for he was unable to say much more about it. Seeing the miserable young stranger

---

[54]W Y Fullerton's is very detailed and interesting; Arnold Dallimore's is more recent (Banner of Truth Trust, reprint 2005) and very readable.

sitting under the gallery, with great enthusiasm he called out to him to "Look to Christ – Look and live!" Charles Spurgeon did that there and then at the age of 15. Now his joy knew no bounds.

He realised that he should now become associated with God's people in a church. His upbringing in the Congregational Church led him to seek fellowship there, but he was unhappy with their practice of infant baptism. He had decided that he should be baptised as a believer as he had found in the New Testament. He sought and received, albeit reluctantly, his parents' permission and then applied for baptism to a Baptist Church in nearby Isleham. On 3rd May 1850, along with two women, he was baptised in the local river surrounded by people on the ferryboat and on the shore. He said, "I lost a thousand fears in that River Lark, and found that 'in keeping His commandments there is great reward'."

His Public Life and Ministry

When he went up to London, his father and others felt that he should get formal training for the ministry. After missing an interview arranged for him at a college, he decided that such training was not for him. He heard the Lord saying, "Seekest thou great things for thyself? Seek them not!" Another remarkable thing is that some of the office bearers of the church wanted him to be "ordained" and known as "Reverend" but he steadfastly refused this, saying that that was a remnant of Romanism.

His work in London went far beyond his preaching. For the benefit of several young men without any basic education who were trying their best to preach the Gospel, he helped them develop their gift by setting up the "Pastor's College" in 1857. These men had a fruitful ministry – for example in London in 1866 they saw hundreds of souls saved and baptised, and 18 new churches established.

Nor was he unmoved by the social needs around him. In the cholera epidemic of 1855 he mixed with the people to pray and comfort the victims. He established almshouses and other measures to try to alleviate the desperate poverty he saw everywhere. He instigated the Stockwell Orphanage which was opened for boys in 1867 and for girls in 1879.

Spurgeon's written ministry was immense, still much sought after and much blessed at the time: *The Penny Pulpit* - his weekly sermons; *The Sword and the Trowel* - a monthly magazine with the subtitle *A Record of Combat with Sin and Labour for the Lord*; also *Lectures to My Students,* and *The Treasury of David* - an unsurpassed seven-volume commentary on the Psalms. These and many others were painstakingly written with an old style pen dipped in ink. In 1864 his booklet on the error of *Baptismal Regeneration* sold 350,000 copies and provoked much controversy. He also put in writing a strong clear warning about the growing acceptance within the church of evolutionary thinking and liberal theology which he declared was threatening to "downgrade" the church – which, alas, it did.

In his huge ministry he was ably supported by his wife Susannah (Thomson) whom he had married in 1856. They had twin sons Charles and Thomas. Part of her work was to obtain and send out good books to over 6,000 needy ministers at home and abroad. She was however a chronic invalid for most of their married life.

Mr Spurgeon himself became increasingly weak and ill, perhaps due to overwork. He suffered severely from gout and occasional depression. He regularly sought relief in southern France for the winter months, but eventually weakness and pain overcame his strong spirit. He preached his final sermon at the Metropolitan Tabernacle on 7th June 1891.

He died in France on 31st January 1892. A week later over 60,000 people filed past his casket in the church where he had preached so often to so many. Immense emotional crowds followed his cortege and attended his burial in Norwood Cemetery. This servant of God who had left his mark on so many died at the age of just 57.

Spurgeon's Bible

Later in that year D L Moody had his final campaign in London. Before he returned to America Mrs Spurgeon presented him with her late husband's large pulpit Bible in which she wrote this inscription:

MR D L MOODY, from MRS C H SPURGEON

In tender memory of the beloved one gone home to God. This Bible has been used by my beloved husband, and is now given with unfeigned pleasure to one in whose hands its service will be continued and extended.

S SPURGEON, Westwood, London, Nov. 20, 1892

This was the Bible in which Spurgeon had kept track of his sermons as they were printed. By means of red ink entries in the margin, he knew at once in what volume or magazine any sermon might be found.

Mrs Spurgeon also pasted onto the flyleaf of that Bible Mr Spurgeon's own inscription from the years he had used it daily. It read:

C. H. SPURGEON.

The lamp of my study 1858
The light is as bright as ever 1861
Oh that mine eyes were more opened! 1864
Being worn to pieces, rebound 1870.
The lantern mended and the light as joyous to mine eyes as ever.

This Bible became Moody's most prized volume. Its presentation to him clearly marked the mutual esteem and appreciation which the two great evangelists had for each other.

BC

CHAPTER 30

The Welsh Revival of 1904-05

One of the most intense and spiritually transforming revivals occurred in what was the vast coal mining area in the valleys of South Wales. It is reckoned that 150,000 souls were saved within a year and communities were changed almost beyond belief. Here are some descriptions of what was happening towards the end of 1904[55].

'Just after 11pm on a Wednesday evening, the words of the hymn "Here is love vast as the ocean"[56] reached the ears and touched the hearts of maybe 1,000 people squeezing into every spare corner of Ebenezer Baptist Church, Abertillery. They had been there for more than four hours, in a service of intense emotion. Meetings like it were taking place across Wales night after night, with fervent prayer and passionate singing - and similar disregard for the clock.'

'The chapel was filled to capacity for a prayer meeting that lasted until 3am. Soul winning spread through the coalmines. Profane swearing stopped. Productivity in the mines increased. Even the pit ponies were confused by the change in their masters' behaviour, coaxing replaced kicking and cursing. Orders from Wales to the Bible Society for the Scriptures were over three times more than for the corresponding period in 1903.'

---

[55]From *The Times and the Abertillery South Wales Gazette*
[56]This lovely hymn (by William Rees) became known as "The Love Song of the Revival".

'The chapel was packed in the afternoon... and there was a warmer feeling in the assembly from the start. Probably this was due to the spirit which a company of colliery workmen - black faces, working clothes, and boxes and jacks - imparted when they dropped into the meeting on their way home... and started in a spirited manner the songs of the revival, creating a fervour which did not flag during the remainder of the meeting.'

'Some deeply intelligent but unconverted men, who had always led exemplary lives, would feel such sorrow of soul as made them tremble, turn deathly pale, and cry out for the prayers of their brethren. Others, very different in their past record, were, even when sodden in drink, so overwhelmed that they professed to be unable to continue in their drunken way, but were forced up to the Schoolroom or Chapel, preferring to wait there until they had sobered than fail to give themselves to the Lord.'

On January 11th 1905 *The Times* noted that David Lloyd-George, later to become Prime Minister, said the Welsh revival gave hope 'that at the next election Wales would declare with no uncertain sound against the corruption in high places which handed over the destiny of the people to the horrible brewing interest'. One of his political rallies was taken over by the revival, and he was moved when a young girl prayed in the presence of 2,000 people. One tavern sold only 9 pence worth of liquor on Saturday night, he said.

The Times also observed that –

'The whole population had been suddenly stirred by a common impulse. Religion had become the absorbing interest of their lives. They had gathered at crowded services for six and eight hours at a time. Political meetings and even football matches were postponed...quarrels between trade-union workmen and non-unionists had been made up... At Glyn-Neath a feud had existed for 10 or 12 years between the two Independent chapels, but during the past week united services have been held in both chapels, and the ministers have shaken hands before the congregations'.

Four years later, David Collier, pastor of Ebenezer Baptist Church wrote:

'Men who had not taken one penny home in 17 years now took all home. Houses became decently furnished, women and children became decently clad. The public houses became practically empty. Bridges and walls, instead of being covered with obscene remarks, were now covered with lines from Bible and hymn book. The streets echoed with hymns, rather than the drunkard's songs.'

'Alas, that so many of the converts have fallen away - fallen away through such causes as always operate; but for the Glory of God and the encouragement of men, let it be known that drunkards, swearers, gamblers of most abandoned and hopeless type became holy men, that backsliders of 20 years returned to the fold, men who had entered only on the profession of religion, entered into its power, and they are with us still.'

Evan Roberts (1878 - 1951)

Evan Roberts was a key figure in the revival, but he did not organise or control it. In fact, no single man directed it. It seemed to break out spontaneously in several places. But it was said that God used Roberts because of his simplicity and spiritual power. He had been a miner and blacksmith with little theological background, but with a heart to see souls saved. He said, "The movement is not of me, it is of God. I would not dare to try to direct it. Obey the Spirit, that is our word in everything. It is the Spirit alone which is leading us in our meetings and in all that is done."

He was one of 14 children born to Henry and Hannah Roberts. The spiritual atmosphere of his home and chapel shaped his life, and he developed a love of literature and music. A devout young lad, he would take his Bible everywhere with him, including taking it down the mine to read during rest periods. One day an explosion took the lives of five of his fellow miners. He narrowly escaped, but the flames scorched the pages of the Bible he was reading (at 2 Chronicles 6). Later, pictures of his scorched Bible became a symbol of the fire of revival in Wales.

During 1904 prayer meetings for world revival were being held in many places throughout Great Britain. Evan Roberts had already prayed for 13 years for the Holy Spirit to control him. He regularly spent 3-4 hours every night in communion with the Lord, until in October 1904 he felt the Holy Spirit leading him to become a preacher of revival. Seth Joshua, a leading Bible teacher, had been asking God for four years to select someone for this task. Roberts went to hear Joshua at Blaednnannerch. He closed the service praying, "Lord...Bend us." Roberts went to the front, knelt, and with deep feeling cried, "Lord, bend me." He later said, "I felt ablaze with a desire to go through the length and breadth of Wales to tell of my Saviour," and this he began to do in late 1904. He said to his best friend, Sydney Evans, "Oh, Syd, we are going to see the mightiest revival that Wales has ever known - the Holy Spirit is coming just now." He added, "We must get ready. We must get a little band and go all over the country preaching." Suddenly Roberts stopped, looked at Sydney, and said, "Do you believe that God can give us 100,000 now?" Within six months, 100,000 were converted in Wales. The influence of the revival was to bring much blessing in many other places beyond the borders of Wales – at Bradford, Leeds, and Nuneaton in England; Charlotte Chapel in Edinburgh; Lurgan and Bangor University in Ireland, to mention only a few[57].

While preaching in North Wales, Roberts collapsed. He was a strong young man, a former miner, only 27 when God used him to such effect, but the burden of his work became too much for him. The rest of his life was spent in seclusion.

---

[57]Useful internet sources: www.openheaven.com www.bbc.co.uk/blogs/wales theologicalstudies.org.uk

During this revival there was much emotion and the emphasis was on the 'moving of the Spirit'. But it seems that there was very little proper and necessary Bible teaching so that the many new converts were not discipled in the ways of the Lord. About a fifth of those saved in Wales joined recently formed Pentecostal Fellowships which began to proliferate in Wales and also in the USA.

Just over 100 years later so much has changed. In Wales as elsewhere the coal mining industry has disappeared, and other heavy industries too. The population has shifted, and the number of 'church-goers' in Abertillery and throughout the UK is a mere fraction of what it was in those thrilling days of dramatic conversions.

It is right for us to pray and long for a repeat of those revival days among us. But let us never overlook the less spectacular ways in which the Holy Spirit still moves in individuals and communities. Let's never forget the importance of teaching the Scriptures along with the preaching of the Gospel. We also need to remember the 'Four Points' which Roberts maintained were essential for personal revival:

> Put away any unconfessed sin.
> Put away any doubtful habit.
> Obey the Holy Spirit promptly.
> Confess Christ publicly.

BC

CHAPTER 31

A Revival along the East Coast

After the end of the tragic and costly 1914-18 war in Europe, much of Great Britain was impoverished and many of its people were disillusioned. The survivors of that war and the families of those who did not return had now to face a seriously changed society. Politicians made many promises like "making a fit land for heroes to live in" but these seemed empty. Many mainstream churches seemed unable to offer any comfort or spiritual hope for the future, and sad to say, many churches had abandoned the true Gospel of the grace of God.

But God was about to move again in a mighty way. There was to be a great revival in an area of the country hitherto untouched in the way that had affected crowds of city dwellers in Spurgeon's time and under the preaching of Moody and Sankey, and as it had among the coal-miners in Wales 15 years before. It would involve another group of hard working people who were also no strangers to danger and hardship, this time on the sea. It would be thousands of fishermen and their families. It was to start in Lowestoft and Great Yarmouth, two coastal towns of East Anglia, and then spread northwards in a dramatic way along a large part of the east coast of Scotland. Naturally speaking it would involve the mysterious migratory habits of shoals of herring harvested by hundreds of drift-net fishing boats in the North Sea. Spiritually speaking it would involve a minister in Lowestoft called Douglas Brown and barrel maker called Jock Troup from Wick in the very north of Scotland.

East Anglia

It was 1921 when the revival really happened, but God had been working in the hearts of individuals for some time before this, on the one hand to awaken His people to prayer, and on the other to cause an awareness of life's uncertainties and awaken a realisation of a spiritual need. In 1916, for example, in a capricious attempt to provoke action by the British navy, German battleships had bombarded Lowestoft and many townspeople had been killed (as happened in other east coast towns such as Whitby and Scarborough). Added to that now was the awful toll of injuries and casualties from the war, and a recent widespread flu epidemic had wreaked havoc among young and old. People were afraid.

In the London Road Baptist Church in Lowestoft there was a godly minister called Hugh Ferguson. He had been there from 1917. Along with a few others like the Port Missionary Peter Greasley of the Fishermen's Bethel, he consistently preached the Gospel and many were saved. His Bible Class had around 50 young people in it every Wednesday evening. For two years before 1921 the Prayer Meeting every Monday evening had up to 90 present, mostly young people, asking God to pour out His blessing and revive their needy town. But as yet they had no indication as to whom God might use.

One Sunday during the autumn of 1920, Mr Ferguson went up to London to hear Douglas Brown of Ramsden Road Baptist Church in Balham whose preaching had been greatly blessed there. He invited Mr Brown to Lowestoft for a week's mission which was eventually arranged for March 1921. Mr Brown agreed to come, but before he was truly ready to take the step he was to have deep dealings with God in private about his own state of soul and his willingness to surrender to God's will.

When the mission was advertised, the local Christians had some reservations - how many would come and hear the Gospel? The venue was the London Road Baptist Church which seated 750 people. It was soon packed to overflowing, as were other churches in the town. Douglas Brown's preaching centred on what they called the old fashioned Gospel of Ruin by the Fall, Redemption by the Blood, Regeneration by the Holy Spirit, the Return of the Lord Jesus. During the first week around 50 people each night came to repentance and faith in Christ for salvation. The arranged programme in most of the churches in Lowestoft was then abandoned and the preaching continued for a month when it is estimated that at least 500 souls were saved. One Wednesday evening the minister in Christ's Church had to ask those who were already saved to go into the adjoining hall and pray to make room for others: 200 left and their places were soon taken by those who wanted to hear the Gospel. They had been praying for showers of blessing and they said God gave them a cloudburst!

There were many remarkable cases of conversion, some involving whole families. As individuals were saved they prayed earnestly for their loved ones and God answered. Professional men came and listened to the message of grace, would-be suicides were stopped on what they had intended to be their last walk to the harbour and were drawn to the Saviour, drunken men who had made their homes a misery were changed by the power of God and joined their wives in finding Christ. Another important feature of the mission was regular afternoon sessions of Bible teaching which consolidated the work and established the young converts. Topics such as the return of the Lord Jesus and the Judgement Seat of Christ were discussed at length. At the end of March the final meeting was held in the largest church in the town, St John's, and every space was filled with many standing outside. The Sankey hymns they sang echoed the message of redeeming love and precious blood to save. There had never been a meeting like it in Lowestoft, before or since.

Douglas Brown came back to East Anglia again that year during June and July, and with the involvement of local preachers the revival spread to Great Yarmouth and inland to Ipswich, Norwich, and Cambridge. In all of these towns God blessed His Word to the salvation of many more. In September there was a large convention back in Lowestoft where revival preaching was mixed thanksgiving and praise, and with tears and prayers for God to do more[58].

Scottish Fishermen

While all this was going on, significant things were happening elsewhere. In the North Sea the shoals of herring were again on their annual migration from the north east Scottish waters off Wick, Fraserburgh and Peterhead during the summer months south to the shallower waters off East Anglia in the autumn. Vast numbers of drift net fishing boats followed the herring shoals, a few still under sail but more were now the legendary steam drifters. Wherever the boats went, an army of womenfolk followed them to gut the herrings and pack them pickled in salt into wooden barrels, mostly for export. It was still a huge industry, although the war had removed some of the continental markets and a slow decline in catches was beginning to show itself.

So in late September Lowestoft and Great Yarmouth became temporary home to thousands of Scottish women whose menfolk would sail from these ports along with local drifters to catch herring. That year the season did not have a promising start, the fish were few and in poor condition, and lengthy spells of bad weather meant that boats were confined to port for days on end. Poor catches meant meagre earnings in spite of hours of toil night and day, while expenses mounted up. That autumn fishing was to be one of the poorest seasons on record for catching herring, but the rich spiritual harvest would last for generations afterwards. Christians on the Scottish boats found good fellowship in their respective churches wherever they went. Unbelievers frequented local pubs or wandered aimlessly at the weekends.

Into such a scene came Jock Troup from Wick in October 1921, a cooper, there to make the wooden barrels for the salted herrings. His work was another necessary part of the industry,

---

[58]More details in *A Forgotten Revival* by Stanley C Griffin, Day One Publications, 1992.

but not too many barrels were required so far that autumn. But his real calling was to preach the Gospel, especially in the open air. The quayside on a Saturday evening offered great opportunities and he took them. Hundreds of ungodly fishermen instead of wandering to the pubs were riveted to the spot as they heard Jock's booming voice earnestly proclaiming the way of salvation. Convicted of their sin by the mighty power of the Holy Spirit, they knelt on the hard ground and accepted the Saviour for themselves there and then. Wives and girlfriends were likewise converted, some unable to continue with their work until the matter was settled. Men at sea who had not already made their decision did so in the presence of their praying shipmates. Those who lived through these momentous days never forgot them.

Jock Troup's day job was making barrels, but preaching the Gospel was more important to him. It took over so much of his time and energy that in November his employer dismissed him. So he joined forces with Douglas Brown and great blessing continued as they preached together. They were two quite different characters but united in the work of the Gospel. They were supported by much prayer - one prayer meeting on 5th November started at 6pm and continued until 11pm with 1500 people present praying spontaneously and giving their testimonies.

A few glimpses of these revival days are worth recording here[59].

On the third Saturday in October, at the first of many open air meetings held at the Market Place, Jock preached with power on Isaiah 63.1. The Holy Spirit convicted many tough fishermen of their sin and need. They fell to the ground seeking salvation which they found in Christ there and then kneeling on the cobble stones.

---

[59]*Floods upon the Dry Ground* by Jackie Ritchie, Peterhead Offset, 1983, gives homely first hand records of many of these happenings.

Some men who heard the message were deeply troubled but undecided. Their now converted shipmates were praying for them, and several were saved on their boats out at sea on the fishing grounds. One man's telegram home said "Saved ... last to ring in on the ship".

Many of the fisher girls were likewise saved at these meetings in the street. Others spent an anxious weekend at their lodgings and were so miserable in their sin that they were unable to go to their work on Monday. Their boss sent for Jock to lead them to the Lord, and then it was all joy in believing, and they got back to their work.

John, a 20 year old man from St Monans, was going ashore for his usual Saturday night's pleasure in Yarmouth after a week of frustratingly empty nets. At the quayside he came upon an open air meeting with Jock Troup preaching. Unable to continue on his way he listened, was convicted of his sin, and on his knees he trusted Christ as they sang *She only touched the hem of His garment* ... He was the first of a whole family to be saved later.

One day the skipper of a drifter was insulted by his younger son, whereupon the lad's older brother gave him a beating. The younger lad then threw himself into the harbour. He was rescued however, and the next day was drawn to a Gospel meeting where his father and brother had already gone. All three came to Christ that night, and by the end of that week the other seven members of the crew of that drifter were also saved.

Back in Scotland

When the boats sailed home and the womenfolk too returned, what reunions and surprises awaited them, for God had been working also in their home towns and villages. Many had been praying for unsaved loved ones away from home at the fishing and God had answered their prayers. As the boats sailed into their home ports the fishermen would be standing on the deck singing Gospel hymns. Those waiting at the harbourside to welcome them joined in, and "Songs of Zion" swelled louder across the narrowing stretch of water – what a thrill for them all! Places such as Eyemouth, Port Seton, St Monans, Peterhead, Fraserburgh, Portknockie, Buckie and away up to Wick witnessed scenes like these. In many of these towns churches were greatly strengthened and not a few Scottish assemblies today have those eventful days as part of their history.

After Jock was dismissed from his job at Yarmouth, he felt he should return to Scotland, where God had already been working through other evangelists. In his home town of Wick, Faith Mission preachers and Salvation Army officers had seen many saved at their meetings, over 120 on one Tuesday evening. In two small villages near Fraserburgh out of a population of 1500, no less than 600 had professed to be saved and most of them baptised in the local burn - just two examples of what had been happening in these fishing communities in the autumn of 1921. Nor did the revival diminish quickly. In the new year, practically all the fisher families in the small village of Whinnyfold found salvation under the preaching of David Walker of Aberdeen. A year later over 400 were saved in Portsoy. In nearby Portknockie, Cullen and Findochty there was similar blessing. No wonder that this revival is still remembered today in these parts of the Scottish coast, traced back to these momentous days at the autumn fishing away south in East Anglia.

From Yarmouth, Jock returned first to Fraserburgh where he immediately began his usual open air preaching. He had hardly concluded his first meeting when he was taken into the nearby Baptist Church where he found its deacons in earnest prayer asking God to send Jock Troup to their town. These praying men experienced the truth of Isaiah 65.24. In that church crowds soon gathered and weeping over their sin found peace and joy in believing. Great blessing followed in later meetings in different parts of Aberdeenshire, as it did when he preached in the cities of Dundee and Aberdeen that winter.

Jock Troup (1896 - 1954)

The life story of the man God used at this time is worth reading[60]. He was born in Dallachy, Morayshire to Christian parents who moved to Wick when he was seven. He resented his upbringing and became an adventurous and rebellious youth. He joined the Royal Navy Patrol Service in 1914 and was drafted to Dublin where he became a typical seaman who loved the drink. But God was hearing his parents' prayers. On shore leave one evening he found a welcome at the YMCA in Dublin. Through the care and tactful interest of Mr and Mrs West who were in charge there he was deeply convicted of his sin. One night he left them saying, "I think I'll get converted." He went back onto his ship, got into the wheelhouse and on his knees accepted Christ as his Saviour. What a change that brought into his life.

In 1919 he returned to Wick where he joined the Salvation Army and became well known for his loud, clear preaching and singing. He formed a friendship with Angus Swanson, another cooper, himself saved in Wick during its recent time of visitation[61]. Together they travelled around many towns and villages in Caithness to preach the Gospel. On one notable occasion at near midnight in the open air in Wick many were convicted of their sin, and falling to the ground cried to God for mercy and found salvation in Christ.

In 1922 Jock was invited to Glasgow and he studied at the Bible Training Institute for two years. He became widely known as an effective preacher, and for around 12 years was a regular visitor to Ulster, particularly in Bangor. He married Kate Black in Inverness in 1928; they had three children Rona, Betty and Ian. From 1928 to 1931 they set up home in Kirkcaldy, Fife where he served with the Gospel Union.

---

[60]Full details in *Revival Man, the Jock Troup Story* by George Mitchell, Christian Focus Publications, 2002.

[61]Angus Swanson (1904-1990) was a well known and much appreciated preacher and teacher among the assemblies, latterly in Aberdeen.

In 1932 he was asked to return to Glasgow to become superintendent of the Tent Hall. Thousands gathered to hear him from the first, many of them the rough and tumble of the city's tenements. Along with his preaching he provided meals for the poor and the hungry who then listened to what he had to tell them. During the 1939 - 1945 war he provided a welcome Rest Home for countless servicemen and women and ministered to their physical and spiritual needs. His hard work affected his health however, and he resigned from the Tent Hall work in 1945.

After the war he engaged in itinerant preaching throughout the UK. He also made occasional trips across the Atlantic where his preaching was in great demand and much appreciated. On 18th April 1954 he began to preach in Spokane, Washington on "Ye must be born again". He suddenly collapsed and died. He went home to heaven while preaching the message he loved and lived for.

Jock Troup was 58 when he died, as was Spurgeon, while Moody was 62 and Sankey was 68. None of them reached the benchmark "threescore years and ten", but how busy and full their lives had been and what a legacy they left. And think of many others with much shorter lives whose stories you have read in this book, and of some in our own day whose apparently shortened lives curtailed what we saw as their useful service for the Lord and for us, and we miss them.

But whether our own years are many or few it is a sovereign God who determines their number. We, however, are called to "number our days, that we may apply our hearts unto wisdom" (Ps 90.12), to fill them with whatever service our Lord has appointed to us as they all did.

BC

CHAPTER 32

Revival in the Scottish Hebrides

Perhaps the most recent revival movement in any one locality in the British Isles took place on the island of Lewis, off the rugged north west coast of Scotland during 1949 – 1952. It was not confined to one part of the island, nor was it an isolated episode. It really followed deep spiritual awakenings which had occurred in the island some ten years before.

Lewis Today

In what can now be sadly described as post-Christian Britain, Lewis even yet retains much of the character of a God fearing society with strong religious feelings established by habit, tradition and conviction. The percentage of people throughout Lewis who attend what may be called Protestant churches is far greater than anywhere else in the UK, although it is diminishing of late. Both the Church of Scotland and the Free Church in its various branches retain strongly held fundamental Bible-based beliefs.

One evidence of this is the continued observance of the Lord's Day as a day of rest and worship. It is one of the things which new visitors to Lewis find strange, though some find it a welcome change! Hardly any shops or similar facilities open on Sundays, and a recent proposal by the local council to open Sports facilities on Sundays was defeated. They found it difficult to recruit enough people to operate the facilities! Many still call it the Sabbath.

In Stornoway, the main town and administrative centre, large numbers of Christians will be found meeting regularly in several different churches. Unique among them is the Gospel Hall in a prominent location called Bayhead, where a small assembly continues to maintain its distinctive witness for the Lord Jesus.

Lewis Long Ago

Because of its remoteness and the hardship of some hours of rough sea crossings in the past, Lewis was largely uninfluenced by events on the mainland. A clan system persisted, and with the barrier of its own well loved and fiercely protected Gaelic language, integration with the rest of Britain was slow. Centuries ago the people earned what meagre income they could from small crofts and some fishing, exploited too often by absent landlords and their factors. This remoteness also meant that evangelical awakenings in other places passed them by. The first Gaelic Bible was not published until 1801.

Up to the beginning of the 19th century most of the Outer Hebrides was unreached by the Gospel. A nominal and careless type of religion existed in many places. This began to change around 1822 when Finlay Munro then Alexander MacLeod came to Uig on the remote Atlantic coast of Lewis. They found the people in spiritual darkness. Although hundreds attended periodic 'communions' they did so with scant regard to its meaning, or to their state of heart before God. Under MacLeod's powerful ministry, great soul searching took place, until in June 1827 at the first communion for two years, only 20 people were at the table. Within a year a great revival affected the region and converts of all ages made up a congregation of 9,000 people who came to the 1828 summer communion. They walked on rough paths over moors and peat bogs, some for up to 20 miles, now seeking God in earnest. This was the first real spiritual awakening in Lewis.

After this, in the northern parish of Ness, Finlay Cook led many to Christ, while in Harris in the south, John Morrison preached in many villages - a crowd of 7,000 listened at one open air meeting in Tarbert and many were converted. John MacDonald, often called 'the Apostle of the North', also visited Harris twice and further blessing followed. The Uig revival had well and truly spread through "the long island" as it is called.

The 20th Century

Before the start of World War I, some parts of Lewis were blessed with a revival of true Christianity and many converts were added to local congregations. Up to the start of World War II this continued on a lesser scale, although there was actually more blessing in the Free Church in the districts of Ness and Point during that time.

In 1939 a significant fresh wave of revival started in Carloway on the west coast where for five years God had already been blessing many with salvation. But now it spread to other areas. Throughout the island large numbers of souls were saved. Here are some comments from that time[62]:

> 'The churches were full, and the solemnity at those services was awe-inspiring, as the Word of God went as fiery darts to the consciences and hearts of the unconverted.'

> 'Both minister and congregation were so visibly moved that the services were veritable Bochims. The law of God pricked the conscience, constraining them to say as at Pentecost, Men and brethren, what shall we do?'

> 'At one house prayer meeting seventeen recent converts were called upon to pray.'

> 'The effect was remarkable – a hatred of sin, abandonment of a former lifestyle, a longing for holiness, with a dread of bringing any blemish on the cause of Christ.'

This revival did not have one specific preacher nor was it only in one place. People gathered in homes, mission halls and churches for prayer and preaching often led by 'laymen'. Prayer became the chief feature of the revival and the presence of God became so real.

---

[62]Source material gratefully acknowledged: *Sounds from Heaven* by C & M Peckham, 2004, Christian Focus Publications.

Then World War II came, and many left the island and did not return. But after it, many men and women with deep desires for God to work again began praying more fervently, remembering how it had been ten years before. When God answered, it seemed to some that the 1949 revival was a continuation of what had taken place in 1939.

The 1949 Revival

In December 1949, Duncan Campbell began a mission in the Church of Scotland in Barvas, a township about 10 miles west of Stornoway. He preached to crowds in packed churches for three weeks and about 100 were saved after deep soul distress. A month later he returned, and with hardly a break the revival meetings maintained their momentum throughout Lewis and Harris for the rest of 1950.

The pattern each day was a prayer meeting then preaching twice in the evening, perhaps in two churches, with the audience from the first continuing to the second. After that, people would not go home so spontaneous prayer meetings followed wherever there was a hall or a manse to hold them, packed to the doors. Many anxious souls found Christ as Saviour in these prayer meetings while others were pouring out their hearts to God. Converts could be numbered in thousands during that year, and the same story could be told through 1951 when Campbell came again and preached during the earlier and later months of the year in many parts of the island. The preaching was soul searching - the seriousness of sin, the reality of heaven and hell, no hope outside of Christ, salvation by grace alone. The spiritual harvest was truly amazing.

Rather than seeing the harvest as a result of preaching, many saw it as a consequence of praying, as in 1939. A particular example is the prayers of two aged spinsters who lived in an old house in Barvas, Peggy and Christine Smith. They became convinced that God would send revival to Lewis and to Barvas in particular, and that the man who would lead it was this Faith Mission preacher called Duncan Campbell. But when he was invited to come he said no, he was too committed to his present work on Skye. Yet these sisters weren't dismayed, they could not take no for an answer. God had shown them he was the man. They and others like them prayed all the more – and of course he came!

The revival began through such praying, and with prayer it grew and prevailed. Prayer meetings were as relevant and important as the preaching - continuously upholding the preacher, and interceding for the lost. Such meetings would continue to 2am or 3am then people would walk home for another hour or two, rejoicing and singing or calling in to a house with lights still on for more prayers. They claimed that they were able to be at their croft work the next morning without feeling tired! And at the crofts or cutting peats on the hillside, prayers and Psalms of praise were heard across the moors. It was said that most of the island was soaked in prayer and the awesome presence of God.

The revival fires began to diminish during 1952-53, although by today's standards the number of true conversions was still very large. During the early years some groups opposed the movement because of their extreme Calvinistic beliefs, and some groups were untouched by it. For many others, however, lives of careless abandon to alcohol were revolutionised to be used for God at home and abroad to spread the glorious Gospel of Christ. For decades afterwards most of the converts were continuing faithfully as members of the Church of Scotland or the Free Church in most parishes throughout that favoured island.

Lewis was another place, another time, where and when God caused multitudes more to triumph in Christ. The savour of His knowledge was again made manifest by His Spirit working through His servants for His glory (2 Cor 2.14).

BC

ENDNOTE

Perhaps you can remember reading the words of the poem quoted in Chapter 23 from Matthew Arnold's *Dover Beach* as he used the imagery of an ebbing tide to lament the retreat of faith in what he saw then as a modern industrial age:

The sea of faith
Was once, too, at the full, and round earth's shore
Lay like the folds of a bright girdle furl'd.
But now I only hear
Its melancholy, long, withdrawing roar,
Retreating to the breath
Of the night-wind down the vast edges drear
And naked shingles of the world.

If that described 19th century conditions, what words could describe the moral and spiritual status which confronts us today with its deeper deterioration in a society which has largely shut God out of its thinking? Or as Cowper wrote a century before, in the opening lines of *Truth:*

Man on the dubious waves of error toss'd,
His ship half-founder'd and his compass lost

The different chapters of this book have described some of the mighty movements of divine grace in several parts of the world over the past 200 years. Thank God that these do continue in our own day, although, alas, not overtly in the western world which has drunk willingly of the poisoned streams of progressive culture, promoted by the god of this age who "hath blinded the minds of them which believe not, lest the light of the glorious gospel of Christ ... should shine into them" (2 Cor 4.4). But now, as then, we know that the Gospel of Christ is "the power of God unto salvation" (Rom 1.16), and God's gracious desire continues to be for the salvation of sinners everywhere. Thus it is "in the midst of a crooked and perverse nation" that we are called now to "shine as lights in the world" (Phil 2.15).

As we conclude this book with its tales of many courageous people of God and their missions, of great movements of divine grace and mercy to so many, will we hear the call to pray more frequently and earnestly, to preach more seriously and sincerely, to live more humbly and godly, to wait more patiently and expectantly upon Him who alone can "give the increase" before He comes again and the day of grace closes?

So very long ago the Psalmist (85.6) prayed, "Wilt Thou not revive us again, that Thy people may rejoice in Thee?"

Can we not pray like this, as so many godly men and women did before us?

Don't we need to?

A PRAYER FOR TODAY [63]

Oh, for **eyes** that can gaze through glory's false blaze
To a world that is dumb in her grief;
That weeps in the pain of sin's merciless chain
With no solace but dark unbelief.

Oh, for **hearts** that would pray in the old fashioned way,
With the souls of mankind in their breast;
Who would beckon His ears with love's ready tears,
And never depart still unblessed.

Oh, for **feet** that will press o'er a world in distress
To bring it the balm of His love,
To all hearts that bleed, by word and by deed
To point to the Healer above.

Oh, for **lips** more like Thine, my Master divine,
All sanctified, purged from their dross.
Oh, for Spirit filled men to tell it again,
The wonderful tale of the Cross!

Wm Montgomery

---

[63]Copied from *Believer's Magazine*, Feb 1945